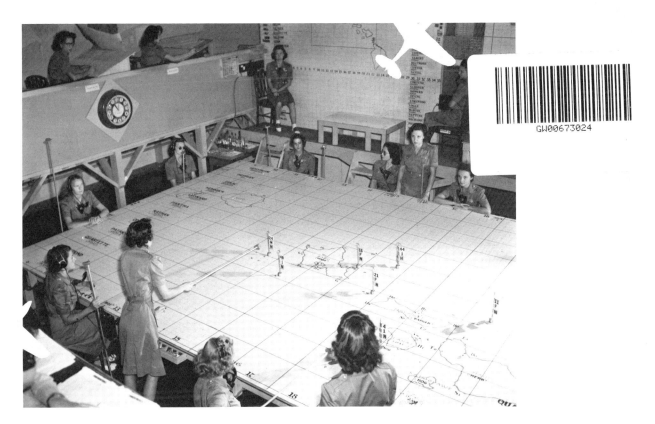

GW00673024

Shuffleboard Pilots:

The History of the Women's Air Raid Defense in Hawaii, 1941-1945

Candace A. Chenoweth

A. Kam Napier

World War II
Radar and Information Center Sites

Barking Sands Field

Kokee
(Radar Site)

KAUAI

Lihue
(Kauai
Information
Center)

NIIHAU

OAHU

MOLOKAI

Wailuku
(Maui
Information
Center)

LANAI

MAUI

Haleakala
(Radar Site)

KAHOOLAWE

Hilo
(Hilo
Information
Center)

HAWAII

Pahoa
(Radar Site)

Kahuku Ranch
(Radar Site)

Opana
(Radar Site)

Kahuku Field

Kawailoa
(Radar Site)

Haleiwa Field

Kaaawa
(Radar Site)

Wheeler Field

Waianae
(Radar Site)

Hickam Field

Bellows Field

Pearl Harbor

Honolulu

OAHU

Ft. Shafter
(Oahu
Information
Center and Radar Site)

Koko Head
(Radar Site)

Foreword

In 1989 I was a student in the University of Hawaii's Graduate Certificate Program in Historic Preservation. One of my classmates was Nancy Oakley Hedemann. Nancy had served with the Women's Air Raid Defense (WARD) during World War II. I was working at the U.S. Army Museum of Hawaii and had a basic understanding of the WARD's story. Our discussions in and out of class personalized for me a little known aspect of Hawaii's military history.

In early 1991 Nancy contacted me at the USS Arizona Memorial Museum to donate a WARD uniform worn by Bette Ballentyne. I was delighted with the offer and planned to use the uniform as the focal point of a future exhibit that would tell the story of the impact of the December 7th attack on Hawaii's residents and of their response. The renewed contact with Nancy and Bette's donation led to a meeting with the WARD's History Project Committee.

It is especially rewarding for me to bring together the WARDs and the USS Arizona Memorial Museum Association (AMMA) under the direction of Gary Beito. AMMA understands the importance of supporting local history projects and making such information available to the Memorial's visitors and agreed to publish *Shuffleboard Pilots*. With the 50th anniversary of the attack that propelled America into WWII approaching, this work is particularly timely. As it speaks from a women's perspective, it is especially welcome.

Kam Napier, an English major at the University of Hawaii, also became infected with the WARD's story and agreed to produce a draft narrative from the material gathered by the WARD's History Project Committee. Kam did a skillful job of reducing a great deal of material to manageable size in a few short weeks. I was able to enlist the fine organizational and editing skills of my wife Candace Chenoweth who produced the final text and made the difficult selection of photos.

Events surrounding the December 7th attack have been detailed in more than one hundred books and countless articles. Few of these resources, however, have touched upon the part played by Hawaii's civilian population and none has detailed the work of the Women's Air Raid Defense, an organization organized in the difficult early days of the war on what was literally the front line of battle. Young local women and military wives volunteered to replace soldiers who were needed for duty on other Pacific Islands. Simply to have made the decision to remain in Hawaii in late December 1941 was an act of courage.

These women were certainly courageous, but what I admire most about them is the joy they feel for having helped their country when it needed them most. They became part of a team that protected their Island home and the hundreds of thousands of civilians and servicemen that lived and worked here. They take great and just pride in the fact that they mastered a highly complex trade and made their own contributions to the improvement of the early warning system based on the new technology of radar. They got to know many of the airmen they served and felt a personal pride in helping to insure that they returned safely from their flights. They paid close attention to the details of their jobs because they knew it could mean the difference between life and death. But, at the same time, it is an unassuming pride and it is born of the confidence that they would not hesitate to do it all over again.

It is an honor to know them and a great pleasure to have played a small part in the sharing of their story.

Bob Chenoweth, Curator
USS Arizona Memorial Museum
Kaneohe, Hawaii 1991

Copyright © 1991
Arizonia Memorial Museum Association
1 Arizonia Memorial Place
Honolulu, Hawaii 96818
All rights reserved.

ISBN 0-9631388-0-4

Editor and project director: Candace A. Chenoweth
Book design: Kennedy & Preiss Design
Linotronic imagesetting: Print Prep of Hawaii
Printing: Tongg Publishing

Contents

Above: WARD Supervisor Kitty Coonley (right) shares the July 1943 issue of The Fighter, *the newspaper of the 7th Fighter Command, with WARD Pat Morgan.*

Right: WARDs Nancy Hedemann (left) and Jean Wilson enjoy a shopping spree in Honolulu in 1942.

"It seems that at last we are really at war. It is now a quarter to twelve, Sunday morning, December 7, 1941. We were attacked, presumably by the Japanese, early this morning. No one knows to what extent the damage is… The radio has been ordered off the air so we are just sitting here wondering what has happened. It's a gorgeous day and all this doesn't seem possible. Everything is deadly quiet now, and I would think it was all a joke if it weren't for the two buildings I'm watching burn."

Pat Morgan Swenson

"As I thought of the imminent arrival of Japanese soldiers in my backyard, I was frightened, but prepared to make a stand of some sort. There was no weapon in the house, but there was a baseball bat that I hauled out to keep beside me. For some reason, it never occurred to me to go to my parent's home for comfort. I wanted to prepare my own home for any further attack."

Nancy Oakley Hedemann

Claire Atkins Becker models her gas mask in front of WARD quarters at Ft. Shafter.

Far right:
Modern day view of Oahu's Kahuku coast from the site of the Opana Radar Station. On the left can be seen the Turtle Bay Hilton.

Pat Morgan, Nancy Hedemann and many other women on Oahu witnessed the Japanese attack on their home. They watched and waited with the uncertainty of tomorrow. Little did they realize that very soon they would be playing a vital part in Hawaii's defense. They didn't know that the radar with which they would become so closely involved already had had its first test. The radar itself had worked very well, but the system of processing the information sent in by the radar sites had not been perfected and failed that morning. These women, and others from Hawaii and across America, would help make the aircraft warning system in Hawaii a success.

Private First Class Joseph Lockard and Private George Elliott had the duty on December 7th at the Opana mobile radar near Kahuku, Oahu's northernmost point. Shortly before 7:00 a.m. the radar picked up a large reflection and the two operators decided to continue tracking the aircraft even after the normal 7:00 shut down time so Elliott, who was training on the radar, could get more practice with the oscilloscope. At 7:02 they began plotting the incoming flight of planes when they were 132 miles north of Oahu at azimuth 3 degrees. After some discussion the two telephoned the Information Center at Ft. Shafter and reported their contact first to Private Joseph McDonald, a telephone operator, and then directly to Lieutenant Kermit Tyler. Tyler's duty tour ended at 8:00 a.m., and the plotters had secured the plot room and departed at 7:00. Knowing that a flight of Army B-17s was due in from California, Tyler made the assumption that the planes Lockard and Elliott were tracking must be the B-17s. "Well, don't worry about it," he told Lockard.

The flight was, in fact, the first wave of the Japanese attack force and Lockard and Elliott continued to track it until about 7:39 when the signal became lost in the reflection of the island. They shut down the Opana radar minutes later and waited for a truck that was to bring their breakfast.

The Opana incident proved that radar technology was effective. The first wave of carrier-based attack planes was successfully detected and tracked. In addition, two radars detected the reconnaissance seaplanes launched from the Japanese cruisers *Tone* and *Chikuma* to search Pearl Harbor and Lahaina Roads (the seas between Maui and Lanai) to confirm the location of the fleet. The absence of plotters and staff at the Information Center after 7:00 a.m., however, meant that Opana's information was not available to Hawaiian commanders. A warning of impending danger was lost.

By February 12, 1942 the Women's Air Raid Defense (WARD), operating from the same Information Center at Ft. Shafter, was coordinating, interpreting and disseminating their findings to all the services. Local women and military wives were assisting in the creation of a unified air defense of the Hawaiian Islands.

For each civilian and each military wife who joined the WARD, the events of December 7, 1941 redefined their life and presented them with new priorities. All they saw and did and felt that day motivated them to participate in the war effort.

Twenty-year-old Patricia "Pat" Morgan typifies one local woman's story. She and her two brothers were born and raised in Honolulu, direct descendants of a missionary doctor and his wife who came to Hawaii from New England in 1828. Pat lived with her mother, an older brother who had just graduated from Stanford University, and a fifteen-year-old brother in a house built by her grandparents in 1903. The family employed two Japanese: Goya, the cook, and Hodai, the yardman.

Pat had returned to Hawaii the previous July after two years at Mills College in California. "A shadowy feeling of uneasiness, a fear

Chapter One

"Sorry, sir, no coffee this morning. Pearl Harbor has just been bombed."

Waiter on board the *USS Lurline*

WARDs
Maili Frost (top left),
Joan Poole (lower left),
Pat Morgan (center) and
Ruth Sykes (right)
take a break from sliding
down the slopes of
Tantalus on ti leaves.

that I'd not be able to return to Hawaii if a war began, kept me from returning to college," relates Pat. Pat's fear was shared by many who had reason to travel to the mainland, and as early as Christmas 1940 parents began calling home children attending mainland colleges.

Since war with Japan had been expected for some time, many islanders were enrolled in civil defense programs and Pat was no exception. She'd just completed a first aid course, a prerequisite to joining the Red Cross Motor Corps. She'd also taken a part time job writing for the *Honolulu Advertiser*. In 1943, to prove that in late 1941 an attitude of preparedness was in the air, not only among the military but among civilians as well, Pat wrote an article describing Honolulu the week before the attack on Pearl Harbor.

"Honolulu was waiting and talking and living…a war town already, its streets and stores jammed with service men and what were then called 'defense workers.' The traffic problem had become so bad that on many streets only one-way traffic was allowed, and confused drivers were trying to get used to the new system. The community entertained service men, and there were parties for soldiers and sailors in many homes… People went to the Civic Auditorium to see Filipino and Japanese boxers knock each other out; they went surfing and to the movies; they danced at the Royal and at Lau Yee Chai's; they read the paper and wondered what was going to happen next. In the legislature the Hawaii martial law bill was killed. Construction on a four-lane highway to Pearl Harbor was begun… Honolulu businessmen were agitated. They wanted a priority office set up in Honolulu immediately for, without supplies, they could not carry on their businesses.

The holds of ships were full of defense supplies. Auto agencies were running out of parts, people wanted to store away food, civilian Honolulu was being pinched by the tremendous war demands." *(Honolulu Advertiser,* 1943)

In spite of her fears, Pat Swenson's first response after being awakened by thunderous explosions and gunfire on December 7, 1941 was to assume that the army and navy were playing war games. A small notice in Saturday's paper had announced just such practicing. When the most violent noise had abated she went downstairs to find her brothers had gone to town to get the paper. Just as she sat down to breakfast, Amy Greenwell, her friend and close neighbor, came running into the house.

"What do you think of all this?" she asked.

"All what?"

"Turn on the radio! It says we were attacked this morning by the Japanese!"

"WHAT?"

Sure enough, from the radio came curt directions, interspersed by military orders. "Oahu is under attack. This is the real McCoy. Keep calm. Stay off the streets. Stay off the telephone." Shortly after, her brothers returned to tell of a bomb whizzing overhead and exploding nearby as they filled the car with gas, a fighter going into a dive, and fire and smoke at Pearl Harbor.

Pat raced upstairs to tell her mother. "We're being attacked by the Japanese!" Sharing apprehensions, the family went onto the roof of their home, as did many of their neighbors, to see what was happening. Pat recalls, "The ocean off Honolulu was full of ships and as we watched more ships came into view, steaming at high speed toward Pearl Harbor. On the horizon a cluster of dots materialized into a half a dozen airplanes sweeping this way and that way like a small swarm of bees. The ships opened fire. Spurts of flame from their guns splashed their dark sides with orange, and high above appeared the black pom-poms of exploding anti-aircraft shells. It was at once exciting and terrifying."

Pat and Amy ran down Ualakaa Street to get Amy's mother. On their way they passed the large white house maintained by the Yokohama Specie Bank for the president of its Honolulu Branch. Each of several presidents to inhabit the house had been Japanese nationals who lived an insulated life, though exchanged neighborly pleasantries with the other residents. This morning the girls noted what seemed an extraordinary sight under the circumstances: a tennis party was in progress on the grounds. There were Japanese men in white tennis attire, one with an eye shade, playing a vigorous game and women watching from the sidelines. Pat wondered if they knew about the attack and, curbing a desire to shake her fist at them, walked stiffly and haughtily by. She never saw any of them again.

They found Amy's mother feverishly digging weeds in her yard. "Weeding is good for my nerves," she said. The three women returned to Pat's house, whose roof afforded a better view, but there was nothing more to see. A strange silence hung in the air. Suddenly the firing started all over again, and again they flew up to the attic and onto the roof. They witnessed explosions at the corner of King and McCully Streets, just two miles away, and near Lunalilo School and Central Union Church, only a half mile away.

Pat started to shake, her legs so weak and shaky that for a few moments she could barely stand. Only with tremendous difficulty could she hold the binoculars being passed around.

The nearby explosions cleared the rooftops of onlookers, and Amy and her mother went home "to collect things." Pat and her family descended to an upstairs verandah, and Pat seized the opportunity to write in her diary. Later she described her emotions in this way:

"I was experiencing for the first time the particular feeling of exhilaration and excitement, almost of glee, which was to last for many days and recur every time the air raid signal went on during the next few years. At times this feeling was supplanted by feelings of real fear or horror or sorrow, but it was there as an undercurrent all the time. It was caused by a youthful love of the dramatic, immense satisfaction at being in the middle of something so important it would affect the entire world, and the queer knowledge that one has an enemy, that he is near, that his intents are deadly, and that one must come to grips with this enemy. It is a sensation that many a terrified soldier has certainly had.

"In the middle of the day we had no idea that thousands of men had been killed, burned and maimed just a few miles away. We thought the horrendous noise was the sound of American forces blasting the Japanese out of the sky. Even so, the possibility of capture was in our minds. We packed 'escape bags' containing warm clothes, blankets, canned goods, canteens of water, and other such emergency equipment. Mother even got out the family 'arsenal,' my father's boyhood .22 rifle and some sort of pistol. We had only the vague notion of fleeing into the hills until the military could recapture the island, if it came to that. The rumor that Japanese parachutists had landed behind St. Louis High School, on the next ridge, sent us scrambling through mouldy boxes for bullets to fit the guns."

The feared paratroopers never arrived, and the family's plan to shoot at the invaders from the verandah as they came over the ridge was abandoned. Pat and Amy went to the Greenwell house once again, this time to listen to the Greenwell's more powerful radio set for more information. They found Mrs. Greenwell conversing with a neighbor's Japanese maid who had talked to someone present at Pearl Harbor or one of the air fields that morning. "Plenty people *make* [dead]! Too much airplane come! He say plenty piece people, arm, leg, on road, all blow up! Too much no good!" the woman cried, flapping the long sleeves of her kimono like a distracted bird. Her eyes shone with tears of apprehension.

As they waited for further word on the radio, Amy received a telephone call from Queen's Hospital summoning her to her civil

Dressed in fatigues, Bette Ballentyne, Pat Morgan and Evanita Sumner (from left) dine at the Ft. Shafter Officers' Club. WARDs were required to wear either fatigues or dress uniforms at all times on the Post.

defense job as a nurse's aid. As only two volunteers had arrived as yet and civilian casualties were pouring in, the hospital staff was desperate for volunteers and Pat offered to help. The girls changed and departed in Amy's car, Lady Cynthia. "I was suddenly very loath to part with my family," Pat remembers, "and when we drove out the driveway I was seized with a peculiar and terrible feeling that seemed to center in my throat and mouth. I realized that this was the 'taste of fear' I had so often read about."

The girls arrived at the hospital at half past four. The hospital staff was concerned with rushing the patients through dinner before nightfall, after which they could not turn on lights. A harried nurse told Pat, "Go in there and see what you can do for those people. When the food comes give the little girl her dinner. She's just out of the anesthetic. She lost her arm. That's her mother in the bed next to her. She doesn't know it, but her little boy is dead. A bomb dropped right on their house." Then the nurse hurried off with, "I'll be back in a moment."

The first bed in the ward was curtained off and frightening moans and cries emanated from within. Another nurse came up and whispered to Pat, "Don't try to do anything about *her*. Terrible mess! She's all doped up."

In the second bed lay a small, middle-aged Japanese woman whose drawn face illuminated with a smile as Pat paused to say hello. In the third bed was the woman's eleven-year-old daughter, placed so her mother could reach her only tiny hand. A white bandage covered the girls right shoulder and Pat tried hard not to stare. She sat in the chair next to the girl.

"Hi. How are you?"

"Fine," the girl said shyly.

"Are you a hungry little girl?"

"Yes."

"Well, your supper will be here in a minute and I'll help you with it. It's kind of hard to eat in bed."

"Okay."

"Shall I tell you a story?"

"Yes, please," and she turned to glance at her mother.

Pat told stories and when the dinner tray came held it on her lap and fed the child with a spoon. As the girl reached for the spoon, the

stump of her arm, severed above the elbow, automatically kept rising and pointing to Pat.

Dinner time ended and Pat longed to get out of the hospital and home to her family but was asked to attend patients on the maternity floor so that staff could care for the wounded. Most of Honolulu's doctors were at Tripler Hospital tending the many injured military personnel.

Later that evening Pat and Amy slipped away. Pat's civilian defense job was with the Red Cross Motor Corps, so after finding blue cellophane to tape over Lady Cynthia's headlights, they made a dash to the Red Cross building on King Street. There they heard for the first time just how devastating the attack had been and that the American fleet had been crippled. They also heard wild rumors of the Japanese capturing the entire island of Hawaii, 216 miles to the southeast. Pat arranged to return home to get her mother's station wagon for Motor Corps work, but as they crept back past the hospital people shouted at them that another air raid had begun and they should turn off their headlights and park their car. "The radio said so!" Rather than wait indefinitely in Lady Cynthia with machine gun and rifle fire sounding very close, the girls elected to make a dash to the cover of the hospital to wait until the raid ended. From Queen's they watched the glow from the fires and the tracer rounds arcing upwards like fireworks in the night sky.

The night was spent in a cottage for interns near the main hospital. The small room was crowded with people who had come to the hospital to give blood and were trapped by what seemed a very prolonged air raid. Occasionally the sound of planes passing overhead would be heard; all assumed they were Japanese and waited for the bombs to fall. "We sat on the cots, hunched, with knees drawn up, trying to make ourselves very small until it went away," remembers Pat. "The sky was a strange color, a mixture of moonlight and fire light. It was a night of sporadic gunfire, rampant rumors, uncertainty, and fitful sleep. When we awoke at day break we felt as though we'd been under continued attack for 24 hours."

On Sunday morning, the 7th, Nancy Oakley Hedemann was up early to breakfast with her husband, Fred Hedemann. Fred was heading the new Trucking Department of Oahu Railway & Land Co. and about 6:30 left home to go to work in downtown Honolulu. Nancy, a senior in the University of Hawaii's Arts and Sciences program, went back to bed to read her assignment in English Literature. Fred and Nancy had been married on Lei Day, May 1, 1941, and were living in a small house on Rocky Hill at Kakela Place, just behind Punahou School, on property belonging to Nancy's parents.

Just before eight o'clock unusually loud sounds of explosions erupted, which in both intensity and duration seemed much greater than the military exercises to which all had become accustomed. The amplifying sound of anti-aircraft firing and a generalized din got Nancy out of bed and she headed to the top of Rocky Hill where a lookout in the former Punahou pastureland was a site from which she frequently scanned the ocean. On her way, she saw her father, George Oakley, who lived next door, starting the hike through the *haole koa* and high grass with a few other individuals who also were curious about what they were hearing.

As the small group reached the concrete platform on top the rocky cliffs, they could see thick, profuse, very dark smoke beyond downtown Honolulu in the area of Pearl Harbor. This sight generated confusion but, as Nancy recalls, they did not deduce immediately that this was an attack. The clamor of shelling and explosions, however, marked this experience as beyond anything previously experienced during mock battles.

"Very shortly," writes Nancy, "three things happened to bring the meaning of the chaotic scene out beyond Punchbowl and Honolulu town into reality. An enormously loud explosion took place nearby and simultaneously we could see a spurt of flames and flying debris from the Lunalilo Elementary School about a mile below, off Punahou Street which leads down to Waikiki. Within moments a sweep of several roaring fighter planes curved overhead in banking formation, heading toward Makiki. Looking up we saw the rising sun on the wings of the planes. Then, a young man came running up to the crest of the hill to say that he had heard from Pearl Harbor that all the ships

and planes had been destroyed and that there was no defense of the island. Hearing this we headed to our homes to prepare for possible invasion by the Japanese.

"My Dad went to join Mother, and I knew it would be a long time before I would hear from Fred, so I made my plans, based on common sense, thinking of all the things to do, as I ran home.

"The radio announcer repeated that the attack was real and that the landing of parachutists had been reported above St. Louis Heights, across Manoa Valley from our homes. We also were told that we should beware of deliberate contamination of the water supply. This information led to a high state of vigilance during the rest of the morning, as I filled the washing machine with water and as many bottles as I could find to place in the refrigerator.

"As I thought of the imminent arrival of Japanese soldiers in my backyard, I was frightened but prepared to make a stand of some sort. There was no weapon in the house, but there was a baseball bat and I hauled it out to keep beside me. For some reason, it never occurred to me to go to my parent's home for comfort. I wanted to prepare my own home for any further attack.

"Blackout began that night and the streets were cleared of civilian traffic. I had a small meal with my parents and returned to my home, telephone and radio. Again we were told not to use the telephone and to remain at home and that a military government was being set up to control the island. Fred finally called late Sunday night to say he was alright, working hard dispatching trucks with supplies. He did not return home for two days

On the morning of December 7, 1941, a half block of shops and homes at the intersection of King and McCully Streets was consumed by flames before firemen and civilians were able to extinguish fires started by an exploding anti-aircraft shell.
U.S. Army Museum of Hawaii

Kathy Cooper, age twenty-one, poses in the WARD's light blue, "sharkskin" dress uniform.

Although dating enlisted men was frowned upon, WARDs were constantly invited to attend functions for officers and their company was viewed as a great morale booster. Pictured with dates in front of the Ft. Shafter Recreation Center are Val Coon (left) and Dottie Dutton (right).

and his work continued daily for two months. On Monday morning we heard the news that President Roosevelt had declared war on Japan. After the sense of isolation created by destruction of defenses and the long day of uncertainty, his stirring speech was a source of relief."

Like Pat Morgan and Nancy Hedemann, other local girls who joined the WARD have vivid memories of that morning. Valeria 'Val' Coon Dotterrer, a California girl working as Director of Home Services at the Gas Company in Honolulu, recollects sitting at the beach at Waikiki watching the blitz at Pearl Harbor. Ellin White Burkland, a Red Cross Blood Bank volunteer, was at home when the attack occurred. She recalls that the first thing she did was wash her hair! Betty Cornwell Hogoboom, daughter of an Island man, was visiting her cousin in Nuuanu. She remembers that an anti-aircraft shell went astray that morning and landed on the house next door to her cousin's.

Accompanying a navy family to care for their child, Dorothy Dutton Montague Beach had arrived in Honolulu in 1939. She began flying lessons and to swim and surf at Waikiki under the coaching of Willie Whittle and sometimes Duke Kahanamoku. She was living on Seaside Avenue in Waikiki and on the morning of the blitz had awakened early in anticipation of a picnic with friends and three Navy officers. The sound of a plane flying over very

low gave her a strange feeling. Then the radio announced the bombing of Pearl Harbor. "Oh heck," "Dottie" thought to herself, "there goes our picnic." After the war started, she volunteered for the Red Cross until she heard about the WARD.

Mrs. Una Walker was head of Honolulu's Red Cross surgical dressing unit. The morning of the 7th she realized that no local Japanese women had reported for work, most of the workers were doctors' wives. Not knowing how to handle this situation, Mrs. Walker called one of her Japanese volunteers, Mrs. Asahina, to ask when she would be coming in, as there were no Japanese ladies. Mrs. Asahina replied, "We'll be there in a minute." Mrs. Asahina later told Mrs. Walker that hearing her voice was one of the great moments of her life because she hadn't known what was expected of her. Several days later Mrs. Walker was awakened at 4:00 a.m. by a telephone call from General Howard Davidson. Davidson asked Mrs. Walker to prepare a list of twenty bright, reliable women to be the nucleus of a secretive Army job.

There was no lack of intensity in the shock, outrage, or sense of violation that the local civilian women felt as they watched in disbelief as their homes were attacked. This sensation took yet another twist for the military wives who realized that their loved ones were Japan's target. In many cases, these women lived on the bases under attack. They knew the Japanese had come specifically for them, for the military presence in Hawaii. Thus the military wives who joined the WARD were powerfully motivated. Kathy Cooper notes, "About half of the original members of the WARD were service wives whose husbands were on duty with the Army, Navy, or Marines. A few were daughters of service men. All were young. Some were wives from Island families. Many were brides newly arrived from the mainland. Most had been living on military bases such as Schofield, Hickam Field, or Pearl Harbor.

"To lessen the responsibility and demands of the military leaders during the turmoil of the war, the evacuation of all service dependents was ordered. Hundreds of wives and children returned to the mainland. General Davidson, however, convinced the top echelons of the Hawaiian Department, United States

Army, that the work of the WARD was so vital that service dependents willing and able to join the organization should be allowed to remain in Hawaii.

"The military wives who joined the WARD exhibited the same qualities as its young civilian members. The thundering explosions and raging fires of the December 7th attack shattered not only ships and planes, barracks and buildings, people and places, but also our way of life. It forever changed our expectations. First on our minds was the strong desire to help the war effort as best we could. The top secret work of the WARD was appealing and an added bonus for some of us was the hope that we'd have more chances to see our husbands when they were off duty in Hawaii. The training and personal discipline involved in being a WARD was, in a sense, easier for the military wives, since they certainly should have absorbed from their husbands a knowledge of appropriate behavior in military work."

Kathy Cooper's unforgettable experience of the attack, in the heart of Pearl Harbor Navy Base, as both daughter and wife to Navy service men, helps explain her sense of commitment to the Women's Air Raid Defense. Her account begins on December 6, 1941, "…a beautiful day in Hawaii."

"I was living temporarily with my family in Pearl Harbor, where my father was on duty. My husband of three months, Bud Cooper, had been in Mare Island Shipyard for the last sixty days. His submarine, the *USS Pollack*, had been sent there for special repairs and refitting, and was due back in Pearl Harbor the next day, December 7th.

"Fairly early in the morning I drove from Pearl to Waikiki, where Bud and I had a tiny apartment at 2244-B Aloha Drive. I stocked the tiny fridge and two storage shelves with groceries I had bought the day before, did some minor cleaning and straightening, and started out in the car to help at a 'Bundles for Britain' group. After that, I drove back to Pearl Harbor to get ready for a wives' party in Manoa that one of the *Pollack* wives had planned that evening. It took me a while to decide what to wear, and I ended up choosing a short dress I especially liked. However, when I arrived at the party, I found all the other wives had on long dresses, and since Bud was the most

junior officer on board, I felt I had made quite a blunder. The evening, however, was reasonably interesting, with a lot of conversation about the war in Europe and the possibility of war with Japan. One of the more aggressive wives said, 'We can beat Japan with one hand tied behind our backs.' What a fatal error in judgement, but I know at that time there were many others making the same mistake. Around eleven, I left to drive back to Pearl Harbor. I was so elated thinking about the next day that I was afraid I would never get to sleep, but I did, quite soon after getting into bed.

"At 7:00 a.m. on December 7, 1941, my alarm rang, and the instant I was awake my thoughts raced on to the joyful moments of Bud's arrival that afternoon. I ran into the bathroom to get first crack at the shower and as I dressed I could hear my two brothers, my sister and my parents getting dressed also. 'Let's not be late this Sunday,' called my mother, a plea she made every Sunday at a few minutes before 8:00. We were planning on going to the 8 o'clock Mass at the new open air auditorium (Bloch Arena) just outside the main gate into Pearl Harbor. After Mass we would have breakfast, cooked by our little Japanese maid, Dorothy. Around noon I planned to drive over to the Submarine Base docks and wait for the arrival of the *Pollack*.

"Suddenly, from the direction of the harbor, came several loud explosions, then the sound of airplanes directly over our house. 'Good Lord, what was that?' called my father as he ran to his bedroom window. Then he turned around and shouted to the rest of us, standing there in the upstairs hall. 'The Japs are attacking. I can't believe it. They're bombing our ships!'

"'Daddy, how do you know?' I yelled, unable to believe what he said.

"'The Rising Sun is on those planes out there!' he shouted again. All of us were standing rigidly in the hall, horrified and unable to move or think, except for my father who grabbed his uniform hat and car keys. He told us to go downstairs and stay there, then raced off to headquarters. My brother David grabbed the phone and called his girl, Darcy Burke, who was living just outside of Ft. DeRussey at Dewey Court. He told her that Pearl Harbor was under attack by the Japanese and banged

After seeing the safety of Hawaii threatened, Betty Cornwell, Ellin White and M.A. Woolley (from left) were anxious to join the WARD and contribute fully to the war effort.

The Lau Yee Chai restaurant, located in Waikiki at the intersection of Kalakaua and Kuhio, was a popular pre-war night spot. Bette Ballentyne remembers dining and dancing there with sailors off the USS Arizona *the eve of the Pearl Harbor attack.*

DeSoto Brown Collection, circa late 1930s

down the phone. (Darcy later told us she didn't believe a word David said until she looked out of her window and saw billows of black smoke over Pearl and Hickam.)

"Realizing we were under a bombing attack, impossible as that seemed, we went slowly downstairs as my father had directed. My first impulse was to run out of the house, since my only experience of a bombing attack was from the movie newsreels that showed vividly what was happening in England at the hands of the Luftwaffe: huge buildings toppling over, sheets of flame, dead bodies everywhere. I ran out onto our backyard patio where only three months earlier I had walked on my father's arm in my wedding dress. A Japanese fighter plane was directly overhead, having just dumped bombs on some ship in the harbor. I could clearly see the smiling pilot, wearing goggles and a leather helmet. A large red Rising Sun was on the fuselage of the plane. I remember thinking that I could hit the plane with a baseball if I had one. However, I expected to be machine-gunned at any minute, because that always happened in the newsreels too.

"Terrified, I ran back inside the house. It was dark and getting darker as the black clouds of heavy, choking smoke surrounded us. My mother had lighted a blessed candle, and we all huddled around it and fervently said some prayers. My mother was extremely optimistic and kept saying that nothing would happen to us. My thoughts were a bit different. First, I thought about dying, as I knew many must be

at the time. Was I really ready to face God and eternity? I did not think so, and distractedly prayed about that.

"And Bud, where was he? Did his submarine get bombed outside of Pearl Harbor? I did not think that could happen, but as I thought more about it, I became convinced that *I* would be bombed and Bud would marry someone else. That thought made me unbelievably angry and determined to survive.

"My brother John, along with David, decided to see if they could help in any way, and off they went, David with his beloved Retina camera over his shoulder. It never occurred to me that I should go with them; fear made me unable to think normally.

"Stunning explosions, one after the other, shook the ground and the house. Deep inside my chest I felt a peculiar vibration after each rumbling roar. Sirens wailed intermittently. I ran upstairs to my bedroom and looked out of the window that faced Hickam Field. There, the flight line was a sheet of flame almost as wide and as high as I could see—like hell itself. Sure that death was imminent, I went downstairs to be with my mother and my sister. Someone knocked on the patio door. I opened it and there stood a very young sailor, maybe seventeen, with a rifle slung across his shoulders, and wearing an arm band that had the initials S.P. on it for Shore Patrol. He said he had been assigned to guard the quarters on the street and asked if he could have a drink of water. He was obviously frightened and certainly I was, and I invited him in. We started talking after I brought him a glass full of water. He said he did not know how to shoot a rifle and that when the attack first started he had been asleep in the new barracks just inside the main gate. Some of his buddies had been machine-gunned as they were going to the 8 o'clock Mass. With the terrible sounds of death and destruction around us, the thought occurred to me that he probably should not be sitting there in the house, but I kept on talking with him anyway. He left after a few more minutes, and I know he felt better. So did I.

"The noise of the explosions and the dark, evil smoke had diminished considerably when my father came back to the house to tell us that we had to leave Pearl Harbor and go into town to stay. My one thought was that Bud would call me when his submarine tied up and I would be gone, so I did not want to leave, but my father insisted. He then told us that many ships in the harbor had been hit, many sunk, and so many men killed or injured. Tears were on his face as he spoke to us—that was something I had never seen before—and I could only go over to him and put my arms around his shoulders. It was then I realized the depth of the tragedy.

"He went back to headquarters, and mother, sister and I put a few things in a suitcase and got into our family car to head into town. The main gate was absolute pandemonium as the Marine sentries tried to get the traffic *into* Pearl Harbor: shipyard workers, medical and Naval personnel all trying to get to their jobs or ships. I knew more than ever I should not leave, but I did. We drove to town. Honolulu was very quiet. We stopped at Our Lady of Peace Cathedral to pray. One of the priests told me he had heard that some destroyers had been sunk. I said, yes, maybe more than that, but I was afraid to say anything more. We drove off to the Pleasanton Hotel in Manoa, at the corner of Punahou Street and Wilder Avenue where my cousin, Trudy Kraft, was staying. The Pleasanton was a typical Honolulu family hotel—open, airy, and somewhat rickety—that served meals to those of their clients who so desired. Mostly single working girls, or families just arrived or about to leave were living there. Besides Trudy, we knew several military families who were staying there, and our arrival from Pearl Harbor generated much questioning about what really had happened and which ships had been hit. We did not repeat what my father had said, nor could we give any specifics since we really didn't know which ships had been hit or sunk, but we did talk a lot—all of us. It helped relieve the tension.

"In the back of my thoughts I was worried about Bud and my father and brothers, but a cloud was lifted and I felt life, rather than death, around us. We had an early dinner since the blackout had been announced. Halfway through dinner, the word was passed that the water was probably poisoned, but by then I had finished several glasses and felt no bad effects. No one else paid any attention to that possibility. A first aid station had been set up in a small room of the hotel, and I volunteered to take the night shift. The hotel was completely blacked out, and another woman and myself sat in the tiny first aid station with a few bottles of rubbing alcohol and some rolled bandages on the table and an eerie blue bulb glowing in the darkness.

"Suddenly we heard a faint whistling, zinging sound that got louder and louder, then a tremendous explosion that shook and rattled the old building. It shook and rattled everyone in the hotel, too, but there were no screams, no hysteria, and no patients for us to treat. I felt very calm. I knew I had a specific job to do in case anything drastic happened, and that knowledge gave me the self-assurance that I hadn't felt during the Pearl Harbor bombing. We did expect that many more bombs would be exploding around us. My mother led all of us women near her room in prayer—the Rosary. Later, one of the girls told me since she was not a Catholic, she could only say 'Remember me too, Lord!' after each prayer. Hearing no more bombs whistling through the air, everyone went to bed. I slept in a cot in the first aid room."

Bud arrived on the *Pollack* on the 9th, only to set sail again on the 13th for his first war patrol. Kathy joined the staff of the 14th Naval District Library as a volunteer, cataloguing thousands of donated books and distributing them to servicemen. Her father reluctantly removed her from his list of evacuees, though her mother and sister were sent to the mainland. Soon thereafter she was contacted about joining the WARD.

Another military wife to experience firsthand the attack on Pearl Harbor was Joy Phillips Shaw. Joy, who became the first president of the WARD, was married to USMC Captain Sam Shaw, Company Commander and Post Adjutant of the Marine Barracks at Pearl Harbor. They lived on base at Pearl in Quarters M-5.

In the days before the attack, Joy Shaw explored the beaches on the windward side, often skinny-dipping as hardly anyone lived there. She often hiked with a friend who worked for the "Watershed" projects and collected native wild flowers. Many Sunday mornings she and Sam participated in NRA pistol matches at the Honolulu Police pistol range. Daily she visited their dog in the quarantine station. Yet over daily activities was cast the awareness of global events taking shape and the certainty that something was about to happen.

"My husband was convinced, and was quite vocal about it, that the Japanese occupation of French Indochina was a clear indication of the Japanese intent to seize everything in the Western Pacific," writes Joy. "We were well known for mounting the soapbox and saying that war with Japan had already started, even though they had not started shooting at us. Now and then, at parties, I would sense that people were avoiding us and our soapboxing.

"Most of our social life was with Navy and Marine Corps friends and neighbors. Our favorite restaurants were P.Y. Chong's and Lau Yee Chai. We did much entertaining at home, especially when we moved into M-5. I worked as a Red Cross volunteer in crafts."

Joy observed dramatic changes in the military presence on Oahu as the attack neared, observations that only served to bolster the Shaws' confidence that war was imminent. "It was well known that after the 1940 Japanese seizure of Indochina the Fleet went to war conditions when it passed the #1 buoy leaving Pearl Harbor channel. Although it wasn't given much public notice in the newspapers or on the radio, it couldn't escape general knowledge that the large tunnel arrangements, later known as Robert and Charles, were under expedited construction. Another dry dock in the Navy

Yard was being built. It was known that large underground oil storage had started. There were more air raid drills being held; there was talk of air raid shelters and civil defense activities. The more exposed sentry posts of the Marines in the Navy Yard were made double sentries, with one sentry to give cover to the other. By the middle of 1941 the Marines on the Islands experienced a large expansion separate and distinct from the shore establishment Marine Barracks assigned to internal security of the Navy Yard and outlying areas. Units of the Fleet Marine Force, expeditionary organizations, were pouring in. An airfield on Ewa plantation had been completed, and a Marine Corps Air Wing had arrived before December 7th. Still, not enough attention was being paid to the fact that the Japanese were on the march and that we were in their way.

"We made some preparations, such as laying in a good stock of staples and canned meat that would not spoil in case supplies from the mainland were held up, and setting blankets aside in a downstairs closet in case fire forced us out of the house. We also laid in an extra stock of whiskey with the idea that it would be low on the resupply list. (As it happened, on the afternoon of the 6th, some friends borrowed from it for a party they were holding!)

"Sam and I were sound asleep in our comfortable quarters when the first sounds of the December 7th raid put us on the floor, each to his own side of the bed. My husband looked out the window and said, 'Joy, this is it. We are at war with Japan, the evidence just flew by our bedroom window.' The unmistakable Japanese flag was painted on its fuselage. Hickam Field was being bombed at the same time. The fence dividing the Navy Yard and Hickam was only a stone's throw from our quarters. Within minutes my husband was out of the house, quietly giving orders as to where I should stay to best protect myself. I did not obey him. Our little cocker spaniel dog was so terrified with the noise and vibrations that she leaped on my back and around my neck and there she stayed for most of the next three days.

"Very soon after my husband ran to the Barracks he sent a runner to tell me to alert our neighbors and to fill all possible containers with water, as it was suspected that the water

There was no shortage of humor among the WARDs. Pat Morgan, Katie Smith, Janet Slausen, Dottie Sicher and Joy Shaw (from left) don inappropriate combinations of shoes and socks and their dress uniforms to "salute" for the camera.

supply would be hit by bombs. One of our neighbors was out on the lawn with her two young daughters and little Japanese maid, all agog at what she probably thought were fantastic maneuvers. When I told her to look more closely and take cover, as this was truly a raid, she was in such shock we had to help her into the house.

"After that I watched and listened from underneath a huge and beautiful monkeypod tree on the lawn. A damaged Japanese plane came through the top of the tree, the pilot was visibly bleeding, it crashed on Hospital Point, not too far away. While I was still under the tree, too stunned to move, a tiny and very terrified man came through the hedge and took cover under some very beautiful but inadequate shrubbery. I thought that so funny, I remember laughing out loud. Then, I thought it best that I go into the house.

"About noon, a Naval officer came and ordered me to vacate the quarters, as they thought the fires would take the whole Navy Yard. I refused to go. A short time later, he returned saying they would take me out bodily if I didn't go on my own. He suggested I take any valuable possessions. For some strange reason I took my sewing machine, possibly because it had a handle and was easy to carry, and the sterling silver. So, with my ever present dog, the sewing machine and my next door neighbor we took off to a house shared by wives whose husbands were on Midway Island. (Later I was to recruit some of the same ladies into the WARD.) All traffic was coming into the Navy Yard, and the Marines on the main gate, who were under my husband's command, wanted to know why I was leaving the Yard. They told me to return anytime and they would let me in."

The ladies left, only to return to Sam and Joy's quarters in the Navy Yard after deciding it was the best place to be. "No one wanted to sleep upstairs, so we made do on chairs, couches and the floor. Throughout the night, husbands brought wives to join us, so that we were wall to wall women. Some slept, some talked, nobody cried. We all talked in whispers. Why, I don't know.

"The second night my husband was sadly in need of a refreshing bath and change of uniform. When he came through the *lanai* (porch) door in the blackout, he stepped on the belly of a sleeping lady, who let out a blood curdling scream that set up a chain reaction with quite a lot of yelling going on.

"Our quarters became a place where everyone was welcome, and quite a few friends came to use our showers and laundry. One senior officer off the *USS Arizona* was in such shock that he had to be helped with his bath. He had been blown through the air quite some distance, even so, he pushed and pulled a number of men out of the water before he was pulled ashore.

"One sight I shall never forget as long as I live," concludes Joy. "I followed a truck load of bodies stacked to the top like logs. Most were naked, blackened by oil, smoke and blood, boys from the various ships."

The first members of the Women's Air Raid Defense ranged from wide-eyed students and young brides to critical, worldly military wives. And yet, whatever their backgrounds, the dramatic change in their lives precipitated by the December 7th attack provided commonality. They all shared the trauma. They all carried scars left by the pain they witnessed or the plans and dreams rent from them. The attack demanded from each woman a response, and the work of the WARD became a means to counter directly the vulnerability each had felt that morning. As they watched the skies through reports from radar stations in the months to follow, these women knew that they, personally, were offering resistance against attack. They were playing a vital role in the defense of their homes and loved ones.

*Army plotters man
the plotting table at anti-
aircraft defense head-
quarters in Building 307.*
Signal Corps, February 6, 1942

*Far right:
Historic photograph of
the actual SCR-270B
mobile antenna at
Opana that detected the
Japanese force on
December 7, 1941.*
U.S. Army Museum of Hawaii

After World War I the United States military developed aircraft detection equipment based on sound location. The noise of an aircraft was funnelled literally into the ears of the operator by large collecting horns. The use of sound was the first practical means of detection and had its best application when used at night to control search lights that could illuminate aircraft for anti-aircraft gunners. The sound locators were limited both in their range and by the relatively slow speed with which sound travels.

On February 29, 1936, after considerable experimentation, the War Department approved the military characteristics for a search-light directed by radio waves instead of sound. This gave the Signal Corps approval to develop radar. Radio waves instantaneously would reflect back to the transmitter from a target and give considerable over-the-horizon perception, a speed and range far greater than that of the sound locators already in use.

On December 14, 1936 the Signal Corps conducted the first tests of its new searchlight-directing aircraft detector and on May 27, 1937 demonstrated the detector to the Secretary of War and several members of the U.S. Congress. The equipment was designated as the SCR-268 Radio Set. On September 10, 1938 the first practical SCR-268 service tests were completed at Ft. Monroe, Virginia.

In 1937 the United States War Department assigned the Army Signal Corps the project of developing an anti-aircraft artillery radar and a "Long-Range Aircraft Detector and Tracker."[1] Initially referred to as Project 12-H, the system entered production in April 1940 under the title SCR-270-271 Early Warning Radar.[2] The SCR-270 was mobile and consisted of the antenna trailer and tractor, operating van, generator van and a stake truck containing the antenna elements. This configuration allowed the SCR-270 to be moved to any location accessible by the vehicles. Electrically, the SCR-271 was a duplicate, but its antenna was mounted permanently in the ground.

1. Colonel Wilfred H. Tetley, U.S. Army, Ret. Personal communication in the form of written memoirs, "The Early Days," p. 3, and "Biographical Notes and Corrections," p. 1.

2. Tetley, "Early Days," p. 3.

By 1940 the British had developed radar into an effective aircraft warning tool that indicated bearing, distance and altitude of aircraft. When plotted on a map, this information enabled a ground controller to vector Royal Air Force (RAF) Interceptor pilots to the location of attacking enemy planes. British radar tracked the Luftwaffe bombers and fighters, some even as they left their airfields, during the Battle of Britain when great air battles raged over England as Hitler attempted to annihilate the RAF and later to break the will of the English to resist. Radar tracking allowed RAF Interceptor pilots to down two Nazi planes for every British plane lost and hundreds of Englishmen to reach shelter before the Nazi bombs came hurtling down. The use of radar information to direct pilots to intercept enemy targets became known as Fighter Interceptor Operations and was a vital component of British Air Defense. Americans soon realized the usefulness of the British system and, drawing on the British experience, began developing an Air Defense System centered around the SCR-270-271 sets.

Chapter Two

"What a thrill, even for a cavalry man!"

Captain Tetley on being assigned development of Hawaii's Early Warning Radar System

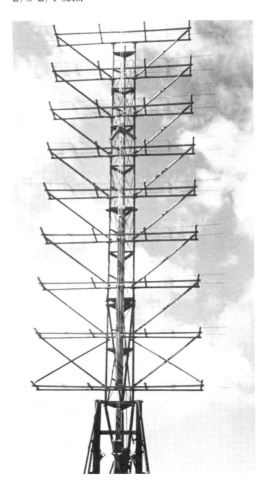

On December 7, 1941, George Elliot and Joseph Lockard saw an image similar to this oscilloscope display that was photographed at the Opana radar site.
U.S. Army Museum of Hawaii

With the SCR-270s and 271s, the signal strength of the reflected radio waves was indicated by a wave-form pattern on an oscilloscope: jagged lines drawn by a stream of electrons on the back of a four-inch circular glass screen coated with a photosensitive substance. Direction was determined by manipulating the antenna to face the strongest reflection. The time taken for the signal to travel from antenna to target and back to antenna determined range. The more familiar PPI, or Plane Position Indicator, "sweep" radar screen that revealed planes as "blips" was not available until later in the war.

In December 1939, Secretary of War Henry L. Stimson ordered the military commander of the Hawaiian Department, Major General Charles D. Herron, to develop an Aircraft Warning System.[3] To do this, early in 1940, an Aircraft Warning Service Board was organized with Lieutenant Colonel George Van Deusen, the Department Signal Officer, as head. Officers from the Army Air Corps, Signal Corps, Corps of Engineers, and the 64th Coast Artillery Brigade (Anti-Aircraft) were on the board. It was a totally new, top-secret project, with many aspects barely, if at all, defined.

Earlier that fall, a young U.S. Army Cavalry officer, Lieutenant Wilfred H. Tetley, then on duty with the Signal Corps, embarked for Hawaii with his pretty wife Audrey on the Army transport USS Grant. "Tet" would be on

duty with the 11th Signal Battalion at Schofield Barracks. World War II had just begun in Europe, and the American flag was painted on both sides of the ship, illuminated by spotlights at night—a foretaste of things to come. The Tetleys were assigned quarters in the Thousand Block housing area of Schofield. Before long, however, Colonel Van Deusen decided he needed Tet's brains and background on the Aircraft Warning Service (AWS) Board and for Tet to serve as commander of the planned Signal Corps Aircraft Warning Company, Hawaii (SCAWH). Early each morning Tetley drove from Schofield Barracks, past acres of pineapple and sugar cane, around Pearl Harbor to Ft. Shafter. There, at the Department Signal Office, Tet signed for top-secret manuals and documents that contained the specifications and descriptions of the new Early Warning Radar System for the Hawaiian islands. "What a thrill," he remarked years later, "even for a cavalry man!"

After several weeks study, Tetley was given the formidable task of overseeing both the fixed and mobile radar systems. Tetley maintained an office at Ft. Shafter to handle the SCR-271 work and one at Schofield Barracks for work on the SCR-270 and the SCAWH.

On April 17, 1940, the AWS Board presented its plan to the War Department. The Aircraft Warning Company, with one officer (Tetley) and twenty-five enlisted men, was to expand into a combat-ready Aircraft Warning Company with twelve officers and at least 400 enlisted men. They would operate six mobile SCR-270 radars. To ensure correct interpretation of the data supplied by the radars, they would be in direct communication with a Information Center temporarily installed at Ft. Shafter Flats. An underground tunnel would house the permanent Air Defense Command Post, which would have as its components the Aircraft Warning System/Information Center, the Interceptor Command, and the Anti-Aircraft Artillery Brigade. Air Defense would be a mission of the Army Air Corps, and the Interceptor Commander would be the overall Air Defense Commander. Later, Tetley would oversee the installation of the six fixed SCR-271 radars on Oahu, Kauai, Maui and Hawaii.

To find appropriate sites for the radar installations, Tetley, along with the officers

3. Tetley, "Early Days," p. 7.

4. Ibid, p. 10. Personal letter from General Marshall to Lt. General Short, March 28, 1941.

5. Roberta Wohlstetter, Pearl Harbor: Warning and Decision. (Stanford, CA: Stanford University Press, 1962), p. 69. Aide Memoir from General Marshall to President Franklin Roosevelt, May, 1941.

and men who gradually arrived for duty with the SCAWH, hiked many miles into isolated and almost inaccessible areas of Oahu. To secure and prepare the desired areas for radar sites demanded complicated negotiations since, in addition to their isolated or inaccessible locations, many were located on lands belonging to the National Park Service or the Territory of Hawaii. Water systems, roads, barracks, power and communication lines, and even cableways, had to be built by the Corps of Engineers. A peripheral cable was installed around Oahu not only to connect Oahu's radar stations to the projected Information Center at Ft. Shafter, but also to serve all units involved in the defense of Oahu.

Happily for the Signal Company Aircraft Warning Hawaii, several competent officers and men soon arrived for duty. Their work days in the field preparing the sites for the SCR-270s were long and hot. *"Kiawe* [mesquite] beans were sometimes up to our knees," claimed one of the SCAWH men. Even more tedious and demanding was the training in the assembling and operation of the incredible and peculiar instrument, radar. Practical application, however, could not begin until August, when six SCR-270 radars finally arrived. (General Marshall had promised arrival by April or May in a letter to General Short.[4])

In a memo to President Roosevelt in May 1941, General Marshall already was calling Oahu "...the strongest fortress in the world." "With adequate Air Defense," claimed General Marshall, "enemy carriers...within 200 miles of their objective will be subject to attack by all types of bombardment closely supported by our most modern pursuit planes... A major attack against Oahu is considered impractical... Sabotage is first to be expected."[5]

The Air Defense that General Marshall so optimistically mentioned, however, was far from completion and by August the military, in general, and Tet, in particular, were gripped by a sense of urgency. The United States had declared a state of national emergency in May and in July sent American troops to replace the British in defense of Greenland and Iceland. Germany had conquered Central Europe and in June launched a massive attack against its unsuspecting ally, the Soviet Union. Hence the majority of U.S. military support was directed to Europe. Japan, having signed pacts with the Soviet Union as well as with Germany and Italy, freely continued its ruthless aggression in China and seized French Indochina (Vietnam) in June 1941. U.S. leaders anticipated that Japan, as an ally of Germany and Italy, might invade Russia or other parts of Southeast Asia.

Army Cavalry Lt. Wilfred Tetley (kneeling left) and Capt. Kenneth Bergquist (kneeling right) pose with a survey party while inspecting sites for the SCR-270s in 1941.
U.S. Army Museum of Hawaii

Since the mobile radars had been late in arriving, Tet ordered longer work days for the SCAWH. The erection, start up, and tuning of the antenna required a sequence of procedures that if done out of turn would damage critical and scarce components. Furthermore, the performance capabilities of each SCR-270 varied widely from site to site, something else each field crew had to learn with experience. The hard pressed and resourceful SCAWH installed the 270s at Ft. Shafter foothills, Koko Head, Kaaawa, Kawailoa and Waianae. One of the radars was deposited at Schofield for training purposes, but on Thanksgiving Day, 1941, Lt. Hogan of the SCAWH, together with a few of his men, set up that particular radar at Opana, overlooking Kahuku on the North Shore. It was a prime station from the beginning and one destined for historical significance.

One area not knee-deep in *kiawe* beans was Mount Kaala, over 4,000 feet and the highest point of Oahu. With an unobstructed 360 degrees coverage, it was chosen by leaders in Washington as the ultimate location for the fixed SCR-271 Radar. On paper it was perfect. Tet had climbed to the top of Kaala as part of his fitness training when he first came to Hawaii and found the mist-shrouded and windy mountain beautiful but eerie. Surrounded by a miniature rain forest, it was also unfit for human habitation. Nonetheless, the Army Engineers had been ordered to begin construction of the site. In great secrecy, they built a roadway from Kolekole Pass Road to the base of Kaala—quite an engineering feat in and of itself. Next, the engineers ran a cableway from the base to the cloud-covered summit—again, a truly heroic effort. The cable car, used to haul up men, equipment and materials, was a ten-foot square platform with vertical pipes around the edge that held a loose rope railing. The main cables supporting the platform were slack enough to have an almost level trajectory at the base that became steeper and steeper as the cable car neared the top.

On an inspection of the site, Tet, Berquist, and two other key members of the Air Defense program boarded the cable car and took off, lurching wildly in the gusty winds as they neared the summit. It was exciting, and the view was breathtaking. As they unloaded at the top, Tet saw that, except for some construction debris scattered around, Kaala was the same as it had been two years earlier. Men and their machines would have a hard time surviving in such alien land, but there was no denying the opportunity for maximum radar coverage from that magnificent mountain top. As the sun was setting, Tet and his group finished their inspection and started the descent. By this time, the exhausted workers manning the cables were in a hurry, so much so that one of the drive pulleys disengaged from its supporting cable, causing the platform to tilt crazily. Luckily, the men already had been clinging desperately to the rope railings as they lurched and swayed hundreds of feet above the ground and the safety devices that gripped the cables in case of a power failure activated. Workers were able to return the platform to the top, but not one inch down. Still, a cold and wet night at the summit of Kaala was certainly better than what very nearly had been their fate. Fortunately some of the riggers who had installed the cable happened to be on the ground and eventually were able to bring the cable car and its passengers safely down. Ironically, a few weeks later the Army discovered that the SCR-271 was unsuited for high altitudes and abandoned Kaala as a radar site.

To receive and evaluate the radar reports of detected aircraft, it was necessary to build a temporary information center, one that conformed to the specifications set by Mitchell Field, Air Corps headquarters for fighter training. The Aircraft Warning Company soldiers themselves built a wooden "penthouse" above Building 307, a storage structure built of cement that was located in the Signal Corps Yards at Shafter Flats. The SCAWH telephone and radio crews designed the interior communications and plotting facilities and worked day and night to have all in readiness for a test exercise scheduled for late September 1941. Inside the Center, code named "Little Robert," was a room almost filled by a table displaying a huge map of the Hawaiian Islands. Large coded grids sectioned into smaller grids were superimposed on the map. At designated positions around the table stood the Aircraft Warning Company plotters, each in direct communication with a radar station operator. The plotters placed a marker on the map for each report that indicated the distance and bearing of any aircraft that came into the radar coverage of the Islands. These markers could be seen instantly by the personnel in charge of the operation, who were situated on balconies that ran around two sides of the room.

In charge was the Senior Controller (Army Air Corps). He was aided by the Pursuit Officers, whose job it was to solve any intercept problems. The Signal Corps Radar Officer, called "Major Oscar," was responsible for obtaining the best coverage with the available radar capability. Any breakdowns or maintenance shut downs meant that other stations had to compensate for the disrupted coverage. An Anti-Aircraft Artillery Officer coordinated the anti-aircraft artillery fire zones. Liaison officers from the Navy, Marines, and Army Bomber Command, and the Civil Aeronautics Administration (CAA), identified flights that belonged to their organizations. This was a chancy identification system, but the only one available until April of 1942, when the Mark II IFF (Identification Friend or Foe) system was installed in Hawaii and on U.S. aircraft.

To accomplish the goal of establishing an interim Information Center at Little Robert, Tetley worked closely with Captain Kenneth Bergquist, of the 14th Pursuit Wing and in charge of the Wheeler Field Air Defense Project. Bergquist had taken special training at the Mitchell Field Air Defense School and pioneered teaching the principles of Fighter Interceptor Operations to Pursuit pilots. "Headquarters at Hickam Field were really ignorant of the value of radar," said Major General Bergquist, years later, "but General Davidson at Wheeler Field was very supportive."

With all the elements of the future Air Defense Command working together for the first time, the scheduled Command Test exercises took place on September 27, 1941. Carrier-based planes were intercepted by the Army Air Corps Pursuit planes with satisfactory results.[6] In November the military conducted more drills. Although problems arose, Lt. Colonel C.A. Powell, who had operational control of the Aircraft Warning Service, sent a note telling of the success of the drills to Harvey Bundy, special assistant to Secretary of War Stimson.[7] It is reasonable to

Brig. Gen. Howard C. Davidson, Commander of the 14th Pursuit Wing at Wheeler Field.
15th Airbase Wing Historian

assume that President Franklin Roosevelt and Secretary of State Cordell Hull also were notified of the progress of the air defense system for Hawaii. For all intents and purposes, the Information Center was now an air defense training facility.

Just after Thanksgiving Day, SCAWH personnel were ordered to their new living quarters at Ft. Shafter. Captain Tetley, worried about the winds of war swirling closer and closer to Hawaii, decided to move his wife and year-old son Richard to the mainland as soon as possible. On November 27, in response to a war warning from Washington, Lt. General Short called an Island-wide alert, designating it as an Alert #1 for the "threat of internal sabotage." That same day Captain Tetley was directed, in writing, to place the Aircraft Warning Service on Alert #2, the threat of sabotage plus the "possibility of enemy sea or air attack."[8] The Alert #2 condition for the AWS was to be in effect from 4:00 to 7:00 a.m., the time General Short rightfully considered to be the most dangerous hours for a carrier-based attack.

On December 3rd, Tetley and Major Berliner, an Anti-Aircraft Artillery liaison officer on duty at the Information Center, received orders to attend the Pacific Coast Air Defense

6. Gordon Prange, with Donald M. Goldstein and Katherine V. Dillon, *Pearl Harbor: The Verdict of History.* (New York: McGraw Hill Book Company, 1986), p. 52.

7. Wohlstetter, p. 9.

8. Tetley, "Early Days," p. 19.

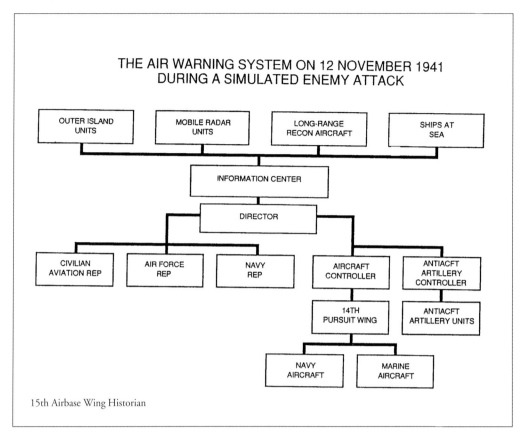

THE AIR WARNING SYSTEM ON 12 NOVEMBER 1941
DURING A SIMULATED ENEMY ATTACK

15th Airbase Wing Historian

exercises. Tet was surprised that in such perilous times the exercises would be planned, but turned over the Aircraft Warning Company to his second-in-command, Lieutenant Norman Tittle, bought tickets for Audrey and Richard on the *Lurline* so that they could travel with him, and embarked on December 5, 1941. Audrey and Tet looked forward to a leisurely and luxurious trip, very different from Army transport style. On board, Audrey soon discovered that many of the passengers were dependents of Pan Am employees stationed on Midway and Wake islands. Sunday morning the passengers' sense of foreboding deepened as the ship's crew began to place rusty steel plates over the portholes, mount machine guns on deck, and begin anti-submarine drills. "Sorry, sir, no coffee this morning," announced their waiter as Tet and Audrey sat down to breakfast. "Pearl Harbor has just been bombed."

Soon the Captain announced over the loudspeaker that Pearl Harbor and other military installations had been bombed by Japanese planes and that the *Lurline* could be in grave danger. Many worries filled Tet's mind as the ship pounded towards San Francisco, zigging and zagging in submarine evasion tactics

and blacking out totally each night. Had the Aircraft Warning Company performed the way it should? Had we made any interceptions? How many Americans had been killed and how much damage had been done? No such news came over the ship's radio. Tet and Berliner knew that they had to get back to Oahu as soon as the Lurline docked. On December 10th at 12:00 noon, they managed to get themselves on an Army Air Corps bomber headed for Hickam Field. Officially, they were waist gunners. It was a trip that no one on the plane would ever forget. The inexperienced navigator miscalculated the flight plan, and when the pilot realized that they were many miles from land and almost out of fuel, he ordered everything possible to be jettisoned; the plane barely made it to Hickam Field. But the devastation at Hickam and Pearl Harbor caused everyone on board to forget their fright. Depressed and deeply worried about the performance of the radar units and Information Center, Tet reported to the Department Signal Office. He learned that his men and machines had discharged their duties extremely well.

On December 7th, at 7:55 a.m., Tet learned, Japanese bombs and torpedoes hit

U.S. ships and planes at Pearl Harbor, Hickam Field, Wheeler Field, Kaneohe Naval Air Station, Bellows Field, and the Marine Corps Air Station at Ewa. Half an hour after the bombs started falling, SCAWH personnel manned all six radars and the Information Center at Ft. Shafter. At 8:30 a.m., Sergeant Merle Stouffer of the SCAWH patched a direct line from the Navy liaison position at the Information Center to the counterpart at Pearl Harbor, yet during the next eight hours and ten minutes, not a single request for information about the Japanese flights or for any other information about the attack was received by Stouffer. As the Japanese attack ended, Opana tracked the departing aircraft en route to their carriers north of Oahu from 10:02 until 10:39 a.m., while Army and Navy planes and ships were ordered to search for the Japanese forces in a southerly direction.[9] When the sound and the fury of that dreadful day subsided, an analysis of the various radar reports made instant believers of the many sceptics in the military previously unaware or unconvinced of the tremendous capabilities of radar.

While Tetley was away from Oahu, the Air Defense Command had been activated and operational control of the Aircraft Warning Service passed to the Seventh Fighter Command under Brigadier General Howard Davidson. Tetley received orders in December to General Davidson's staff as Signal Officer. One of his main duties was the completion of the fixed SCR-271 radar system. Kokee on Kauai, Haleakala on Maui, and Pahoa on Hawaii were the sites, and the Corps of Engineers worked feverishly to construct underground tunnels that, according to recent bomb-proofing specifications, had to be at least forty feet underground. They contained space for three generators, three transformers, radar, ventilating equipment, and living area for the

Prior to June 1942, General Davidson (left) poses with (from left) WARD Supervisor Gwen Williams, WARD Joy Shaw, and Major General Clarence Tinker, Commander of the Hawaiian Air Force.

personnel. A hundred-foot tower above ground held the radar antenna. The fixed 271 sites presented quite a contrast to those of the truck-mounted mobile 270s with their pup tents for the personnel.

Tet also was responsible for logistical support for the AWS and expected to supply all trained technical support. On Christmas Day, 1941, Tet learned that the male Signal Corps plotters, who had served so well during the traumatic early days of the Information Center, were to be replaced by local women. This decision had been influenced by the successful use of the Women's Auxiliary Air Force in Britain.

Although during the course of the war many women filled vacancies in industry left by men, as symbolized by "Rosie the Riveter," few women had the opportunity to participate in military operations that directly affected the defense of U.S. territory. It was a unique set of circumstances that put members of the Women's Air Raid Defense in a position to do just that.

9. Gordon Prange, with Donald Goldstein and Katherine Dillon, *At Dawn We Slept.* (New York: McGraw Hill Book Company, 1981), p. 564.

WARD Jane Lackey
on duty at Lizard.
Signal Corps, December 1942

Tetley and the other SCAWH men were shocked by this unprecedented replacement of active-duty military men with civilian women. Regardless, General Davidson had taken the lead and in order to round up twenty reliable and trustworthy young women to work at the Information Center, had called Mr. and Mrs. Alexander Walker at 4:00 a.m. one mid-December morning to ask for names.

Mrs. Una Walker had lived in Hawaii for many years and donated long hours at the Red Cross. Currently she was a volunteer for the surgical dressing unit. Una was acquainted with many young women and, with her husband's help, had a list for Davidson when he called back an hour later. A meeting for possible recruits was arranged for December 26th at the Royal Hawaiian Hotel.

The military had taken over the celebrated pink hotel and officials hurried about the lush lawns and exotic plants. Barbed wire was strung along the beautiful, white sands of Waikiki Beach to deter a possible invasion. Upstairs, in a suite facing the ocean, General Davidson addressed the interested young women of Honolulu including Catherine "Kitty" Coonley, Mary Erdman, Kathleen "Kak" Lowrey Hamlin, Shada Pflueger, Sybil Scribner, Winifred "Bam" Sperry, Barbara Thompson, Ellin White, Gwendolyn Williams and Jean Wilson. Mrs. Walker was there, along with Mrs. John Howard, another personal friend of General Davidson. Brigadier General Davidson and Major Lorry Tindal explained that women were needed to relieve men ordered to forward combat areas and the duties and demands that the secret work entailed. Their speeches gave the women courage and inspired them to serve in defense of the Islands. The women signed on and the Women's Air Raid Defense was formed. Gwen Williams was appointed Chief Supervisor. Several names for the organization were proposed; the new recruits rejected the name "Women's Air Defense" because they didn't want to be called WADs!

Ellin White was placed in charge of recruiting efforts, conducted entirely word of mouth. The new WARDs were asked to call friends who might be interested in joining, but recruiting standards were high. Applicants had to be between the ages of twenty and thirty-four and childless. They had to pass a physical and Army Intelligence examination and be willing to work shifts around the clock. They also would be required to live in Army quarters at Ft. Shafter and abide by special regulations. An air of secrecy surrounded the endeavor and those asked to join weren't given specifics; they only knew that they would be doing critical work for the Army.

Almost immediately General Davidson realized that the number of eligible local women would be insufficient to staff the Information Center and arranged to have military wives and daughters who fulfilled the requirements taken off the evacuation lists if they wished to join the WARD. A group of Island women whose husbands were in military services applied immediately; additionally, a small group of local women, referred to as the "Town Reserves," were trained as substitutes and allowed to live in Honolulu.

Officially, the WARD was a detachment of Company A, Signal Aircraft Warning Regiment, Special. Executive Order #9063 covered their appointment. The chain of command was:

1. Commanding General, Hawaiian Department
2. Commanding General, 7th Air Force
3. Commanding General, 7th Fighter Command
4. Commanding Officer, 515th, Signal Aircraft Warning Regiment, Special
5. Commanding Officer, Company A, 515th, Signal Aircraft Warning Regiment, Special

Soon thereafter the women were appointed civil service employees. Many who signed up in the beginning were under the impression that they would be supplied their uniforms, quarters, and meals, but be paid only $60 a month. This soon was changed to $120 a month with quarters alone being furnished, and eating privileges at the Ft. Shafter Officers' Mess costing about $32 per month were extended whether or not the girls ate there. Later this arrangement was adjusted so the WARDs could eat a la carte. Their status remained as such until June 13, 1943, when they were detached from the Signal Corps to become the WARD unit of the 17th Fighter Command.

Chapter Three

"A friend called and asked if I would be interested in doing important, top-secret work for the Army."

Military wife
Kathy Bruns Cooper

A young, local National Guardsman stands watch in front of Honolulu's Iolani Palace soon after the Japanese attack. The first WARDs trained at the Palace in January 1942.

U.S. Army Museum of Hawaii

Little Robert, the temporary Information Center/Air Defense Command where the WARDs plotted from February until May 1942, was constructed on top of a concrete warehouse at Ft. Shafter, Building 307, in late 1941.

U.S. Army Museum of Hawaii

The day after the attack, Iolani Palace was taken over by the military government after the declaration of Marshall Law. Here, on January 1, 1942, in a large room that had shortly before served as the Territorial Senate Chamber, WARD training began. Blackout boxes covered several sections of the windows. A simulated plotting board was placed on a large table in the center of the room. Metal chairs were arranged around the table, and a headset with earphones and a mouthpiece attached was placed at each training station. Before leaving the recruits were issued gas masks, helmets and NON-COMBATANT arm bands.

Lieutenant Ardie Konkle of the SCAWH trained groups of women in the techniques of aircraft plotting for two weeks at a time in two hour segments. A hypothetical radar report from one of the six Oahu radar stations was phoned to one of the trainees. In turn, the trainee placed a small, colored plastic arrow on

the map that indicated the location of the aircraft detected by the radar. Consecutive plots showed the speed and direction of the flight. "Rascal" was the code name for the plotters and "Oscar" the code name for the radar operators.

On January 12, 1942 Jean Wilson, Shada Pflueger, and Sybil Scribner met Maria Parker and Barbara Thompson at Iolani Palace. They proceeded by car to Ft. Shafter to work the first shift of evening duty. At King and School Streets they were joined by Martha Greenwell, Mary Louise Weller and Major Kenneth Bergquist, U.S. Air Corps officer in charge of training the pilots of the 14th Pursuit Wing in interception techniques. They drove with several other WARDs into Ft. Shafter to obtain security clearance to enter Little Robert, the code name for the Information and Control Center (ICC) of the Air Defense Command.

The ICC was a new, wood frame, two-story building placed atop a concrete storage structure, Building 307, at Ft. Shafter mud flats. All of the surrounding buildings were inconspicuous structures such as warehouses or storage sheds. Over the mud, slotted duck walks stretched from the road to the doorways of the buildings. No one suspected that up the short flight of stairs was an important link in the defense of the Islands!

Inside Little Robert, past a door draped with old Army blankets to keep light from showing at night and through a blackout passageway, was a large room almost filled by a huge table upon which lay the now-familiar map of the Hawaiian Islands. Plotting stations were located along all four sides of the map table. Above, on a balcony that ran around two sides of the room, sat the Senior Controller (the Army Air Corps officer in charge of operations) and next to him liaison officers from the Army, Navy, Marines and Civil Aeronautics Administration. It was the responsibility of these officers to identify every flight that was plotted. If the flight could not be identified, the Senior Controller sounded the air raid alarm. Fighter interceptors would then be dispatched from the appropriate Army air fields.

Torrential rains soaked the first shift of WARDs as they hurried across the slippery path to Little Robert. Each WARD replaced a young soldier on duty and adjusted her headset as she had been instructed. Soon they heard the voice of a radar operator: "Rascal, this is Oscar. Can you read me?" Rascal responded, "I read you loud and clear," and plots went on the map. The WARDs had began the work that General Davidson had told them would be the most important done by any woman in the nation. It was, in fact, the first time in U.S. history that women officially replaced active duty combat soldiers without a mandate or approval from Congress. The men they replaced moved on to advanced areas for whose air defense the Hawaiian Commander was then responsible, such as Fiji and New Caledonia.

The 104 members of the Women's Air Raid Defense moved into their Ft. Shafter quarters on February 1, 1942, and took over duty around the clock. It was necessary to transport the women to Little Robert in Army trucks, and with full blackout conditions, night drives were harrowing as were the blind negotiations of the slippery walkways. This was the WARD's nerve wracking routine for over four months. Finally, on May 12th, the Information and Control Center moved to its permanent location, a tunnel complex under a hillside at Ft. Shafter—code name Lizard. From then on the WARDs could walk to work as the camouflaged entrance to the tunnel was just a short distance up the hill from their quarters.

Immediately, the question of working hours came up. Because of underground work and inadequate eating facilities at Lizard, Major D. B. Flickinger, M.D., advised that the WARD work no more than six hours a day. After many experiments with schedules, a 6 1/4 hour working day was established. To comply with the civil service forty hour a week minimum requirement, the six hour shift changed hours of work every second day, and WARDs received a 36-hour break every eight days.

Lizard was enormous and had many rooms, but the main plotting room was the focus of activity. Offshoots of the main room had radio equipment set up to receive information from neighbor island radar installations. Another room was used for the training of WARD filterers whose job it was to edit extraneous plots and clarify flights.

One room was reserved for the WARD lounge. The sofas and chairs were usually

Gas masks slung over the shoulder with helmets attached, Fluff Ford, Mary Bullard and Pat Morgan (from left) get ready to climb aboard Army transport to Little Robert. WARDs who served in early 1942 have vivid memories of harrowing night rides under blackout conditions.

occupied by catnapping WARDs on break from the plotting board, but the women were not above sleeping on the floor if necessary. The cheeriest area of Lizard was the snack bar; it was set up in the hallway that led to the western exit of the tunnel.

Generally, the first position held by a WARD was plotter. The plotter's job was to receive reports from a radar site and to note them by placing a plastic arrow on the master plotting board. As successive reports were received, additional plastic arrows indicated course and speed of the as yet unidentified contact or "bogie." Once confirmed as a flight, an identifying marker standard was placed near the flight. This basic skill was the focus of the earliest training sessions at Iolani Palace.

With more experience, a WARD was promoted to senior plotter. WARD experience, however, was not limited to plotting. The correct interpretation of the radar plots and the administration of the WARD entailed a host of other responsibilities. In the December 1944 issue of *Scope Dope*, voice of the WARD, Filter Supervisor Mary Jane Tuttle outlined these other positions in an article for

Several WARDs including Tanya Widrin (flower in hair) and, to her left, Mildred Twelt visit with War Correspondent Larry Bachman (far right) in Lizard's snack bar.

WARDs placed coded chits such as these on a standard to identify the flights they plotted.

the regular feature "From Rascal to Oscar." Tuttle's article also gives insight into the mood and tone of the work done by the WARDs; the language is official, precise and professional.

"Continuing from last month our article on the specialized jobs performed by the Women's Air Raid Defense organization at the Oahu ADCC [Air Defense Command Center], we find ourselves with a girl who has just been promoted to the status of a senior plotter," begins Mary Jane. "This means she's not only been here for some time but has proven proficient in one or more capacities."

"Now she's ready to take a try at an even more highly specialized job which inherently not only demands complete familiarity with the work but intensive training and application in this particular field. This is filtering. The filterer's primary job is to take the information at her command, interpret it correctly, and display it accurately and rapidly. By reasoning based upon the principles evolved from radar operations, time computations, scientific analysis and experience, she should be able to take unconnected plots and read an intelligible interpretation into them.

"First of all she must know the physical location of each station in our area so that with each plot she may compensate for the inaccuracies of the azimuth. Range is simply the distance from the station to the plot, and one of the first things that the trainee filterer hears is, 'Don't change your range—it's accurate.'

However, the azimuth or the bearing of the plot from the station is inaccurate and she can change that, or filter it as we call it. Thus putting this into practice she finds that if she has two plots which fall from two different stations at the same time on the same flight, she knows that the true position is where the two range arcs intersect. This is called a range cut. When working with readings from a PPI scope, she learns that these are accurate in both range and azimuth, and she'll have no occasion to change her azimuth as she would with readings from a SCR-271.

"Next she learns that in general practice an aircraft flies in a constant direction at a constant speed for a certain period of time. She knows the approximate speed of the various aircraft and how large an area on our board a flight should cover during a certain interval. Thus, by the use of range cuts and range differences, established flight directions, and accurate estimates of speed she is able to establish her flights and maintain them.

"Beyond this there are many things she must know. She learns the principles of IFF [Identification Friend or Foe] response, operation and tendencies, flight priorities, a large number of codes, how to handle distress [planes in trouble] and interceptions, how to handle divergent echo interpretation reports, when to have an area raid [air raid], and how to handle radar countermeasures. These are only an idea of the things she must know, and it actually takes several months for a girls to be trained well enough to be capable of handling all her traffic with ease.

"When a girl is deemed qualified and capable as a filterer, she receives a red bar with a blue stripe which she wears on her collar. Each shift has a senior shift filterer who has a red bar with a white stripe, and she is responsible for the calibre of filtering on her shift. There is also the filter supervisor who teaches the classes for trainee filterers and is the supervisor of filtering on all shifts.

"Another specialized job which demands complete knowledge of the entire organization is the one which handles the personnel and this is the shift captain. It is her responsibility to see that the girls are at work and are capable of doing the jobs to which she assigns them. She rotates the plotters around the board from one station to another and from one specialized job to another. She maintains discipline in the operations room and sees that her shift is quiet, orderly, and well-behaved at all times. She arranges reliefs, schedules, and days off. She keeps a Shift Captain's Log showing assignments for personnel, and times and positions, which is kept for future reference.

"The shift captain has an assistant who takes over her position when she is out of the room or has a day off. The shift captain wears a double red bar on her collar, and her assistant wears the finance insignia painted red.

"At the top of the organization is the group which comprises the office staff. There is a chief supervisor who, as the title implies, supervises everything executed by and related to the entire organization. She is our representative to the Army and at various meetings where our representation is needed. We have an operations supervisor and her assistant who handle matters pertinent to operations, shift supervision, and the training of new girls. On their shoulders fall the responsibility of overall efficient operation. We have two girls who handle administrative matters including 201 [personnel] files, correspondence, releases, furloughs, etc. There is the personnel supervisor who is responsible for housing, moving, inventories, supplies, utilities, etc. Another staff member takes care of the miscellaneous items such as local transportation, mail delivery, laundry, and newspapers. We have a payroll department in the charge of our only non-WARD employee which makes out the checks, and takes out deductions and bonds. She has two assistants who are WARDs. There is a resident supervisor who answers the phone at night and handles messages for the girls. She also pays sick calls in the morning. The chief supervisor wears on her collar the insignia of a full Colonel and the operations supervisor wears a red Major's leaf. The remaining staff wear a double red bar."

WARD administrator Bertha Bloomfield-Brown (center) reviews procedures with Pat Morgan (left) and Louise Carpenter in the summer of 1942. Note the Captain's bars, signifying staff, on Bertha's lapel.

WARD RANKS AND INSIGNIAS

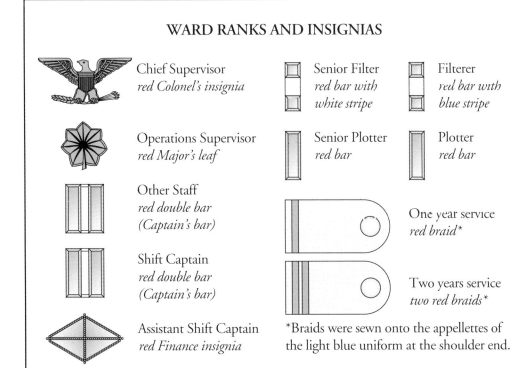

Chief Supervisor
red Colonel's insignia

Operations Supervisor
red Major's leaf

Other Staff
*red double bar
(Captain's bar)*

Shift Captain
*red double bar
(Captain's bar)*

Assistant Shift Captain
red Finance insignia

Senior Filter
*red bar with
white stripe*

Filterer
*red bar with
blue stripe*

Senior Plotter
red bar

Plotter
red bar

One year service
red braid*

Two years service
two red braids*

*Braids were sewn onto the appellettes of the light blue uniform at the shoulder end.

Kitty Coonley (left), chief supervisor of the Oahu unit from 1943, discusses scheduling with Operation's Supervisor Bette Knouse. Kitty wears the full Colonel's insignia of the eagle, while Bette's rank is indicated by a red Major's leaf.

Helmets on and gas masks in tow, WARDs Ruth Sykes, Joyce Knudsen, June Rutland and Wilma Bird (from left) smile for the camera at Ft. Shafter quarters.

"Thus we have the sum total of all the jobs performed by members of our organization," concludes Mary Jane, "and by smooth coordination between them all, each contributes its own important part in maintaining the security of our area."

The WARDs' quarters on Ft. Shafter were located in "officers' country," and an odd combination of military rules and civilian independence prevailed "on campus." Though the women had privileges at the Officers' Mess, they often chose to cook in their quarters. Especially for the younger WARDs who were on their own for the first time, it was fun to experiment in the kitchen and to prepare—or burn—suppers for friends. In great demand for parties, dances and picnics at military

Wearing a headset and holding a plotting rake, Katie Smith sits at the plotting table poised for action. This image of Katie and Dottie Sicher was used as a public relations photograph by Col. Lorry Tindal while recruiting for the WARD in San Francisco.
Signal Corps

installations and private homes, the women had extremely busy social lives on top of a demanding work schedule. Nonetheless, many WARDs became involved in a variety of volunteer activities.

Like their vivid memories of the attack on Pearl Harbor, the women of the WARD remember quite well their first involvement with the organization: how they heard about it, with whom they associated, and what they experienced in those unsettled early days. For many, the WARD was exactly what they were looking for.

Nancy Hedemann's introduction to the WARD came via a close friend. "Right after Christmas, I recall receiving a telephone call from Jean Wilson, who asked if I would be interested in working on a secret project for the U.S. Army which she had just heard about at a meeting at the Royal Hawaiian Hotel. Since I was curious, she told me to appear at Iolani Palace on January 1st to learn more about it. All schools had been closed immediately after the seventh of December so my studies were interrupted and the need to contribute to the defense of the Islands was compelling. Fred was working virtually all his waking hours, so he encouraged me to find out what the project with the U.S. Army might be.

"When we gathered in the Mauka-Ewa room of Iolani Palace, the Senate Chamber, which had been barricaded and draped with blackout materials, I found friends whom I had known at Punahou School and the University of Hawaii: Bette Ballentyne, Jean Wilson, Kathy Bruns Cooper, Pat Morgan were among those whom I recognized immediately. The proposal made by General Howard Davidson was simple: he intended to replace the Signal Corps male plotters in the Command Center with young women from the civilian population. He stated that he needed the men for other combat duty work and wanted to begin training of the civilian women immediately.

"During the first meeting it was explained that the WARDs would be paid a salary by the U.S. Army, be quartered at Ft. Shafter, wear uniforms and be considered officers so that in the event of capture by the enemy, they would be treated according to the agreements of international law regarding prisoners of war. The secrecy of the work and the importance of the activity to the defense of our country were stressed. For myself and the other Island girls, it was the defense of our homes which came clear, then service to our country.

"Fred and I talked about the importance of this work and agreed that I should sign up. His work, always primary for him, had become consuming. Although the WARDs were to be quartered at Ft. Shafter, the shifts were to be rotated, so I anticipated being able to be at home frequently. Fred drove a company car and had replaced his Model A Ford with a pale green Oldsmobile convertible when we married, so I would be fairly mobile within the limits of gasoline rationing and curfew regulations.

"At our first meeting on January 1st, we were introduced to our WARD supervisors, who were modeling the uniforms for which we were to be fitted for fatigue and dress apparel. Gwendolyn Williams was the Chief Supervisor; Mary Erdman was her assistant. We were formally identified to the extent possible and signed up for duty. A photographer from U.S. Army Hawaiian Department photographed me then; later an identification office was established for civilians in the basement of Kawaihao Church. I was issued a badge (#16) to wear while on duty, which commenced immediately. We were issued gas masks and helmets, which in case of emergency were to be kept with us going to and from duty and carefully stored while working.

"The training at Iolani Palace took place for two hours a day in the same room in which we had been addressed by General Davidson. Major Lorry Tindal and Lt. Ardie Konkle from the U.S. Army Signal Corps were involved in the training of the new recruits. Major Tindal's step-daughter, Rae Roehm, had some experience in plotting, so she moved into the organization with previous knowledge. Lt. Konkle lectured and a Staff Sergeant observed and assisted us in accurately placing the marks to represent the track of an object that had appeared on a radar screen at one of the receiving units.

"A large square plotting board was marked by a grid with numerals on the vertical axis and code names in alphabetical order on the horizontal axis. Head-sets with earphones and mouthpieces were attached to stations along the board into which we plugged to receive messages. We practiced receiving radar readings from 'Oscars' who were conveying messages to us, the 'Rascals.' To place a reading on the plotting board, we took a colored arrow and with a poker-like, rubber-tipped implement placed the arrow at the reading transmitted by Oscar. The arrows were red, blue and green; the color designated the five-minute interval of a quarter hour in which a reading had been received.

"Mary Erdman led a six-hour shift through the first real experience on January 12th, then, by the 15th, two day shifts were taken by truck under close cover to the Command Center of the Signal Corps. We knew the Center as 'Little Robert.' This well-camouflaged, highly unlikely structure was approached from the end of the pavement, where transport stopped, by a wooden walkway of perhaps fifty yards distance. At first, until our quarters were ready in February, WARDs were transported from Iolani Palace to Little Robert by truck. The vehicle had closed flaps at the rear to hide the passengers. We were in blue uniforms by then."

In those early hectic war days, supervisor Mary Erdman's calm, self-assured manner was a blessing. She had been doing volunteer work for the Red Cross in a home in Kahala when contacted by an Army lieutenant and asked to work for a new organization of women. She accepted the position of supervisor and immediately began her duties. She learned to plot at Little Robert, then helped to gather a group of women to staff the organization. Gwen Williams already had been chosen as Chief Supervisor, and Mary joined her and several other women to help bring direction to the organization. One of Mary's first duties was to set up shifts. She recalls with a chuckle that although she wanted to be sure that all the women had the times and dates correct and in the best order for all, she had no idea how to go about it. Fortunately, a friendly neighbor who was the president of a large Island firm volunteered to show her how to do scheduling.

"During that first two-week period in January 1941," Nancy Hedemann grimaces, "frequent air raid alarms were heard and, on each occasion, the possibility of a repetition of

The WARDs were given I.D. badges to gain entry onto Ft. Shafter or into the Information Center; girls often wore the badges pinned underneath a pocket flap. After three months of efficient duty a WARD earned the privilege of wearing the coveted WARD wings above her left breast pocket.

Val Coon, dietician and housekeeping supervisor for the WARD until September of 1943, was a familiar face to most everyone on Post.

Patsu Bentley, Carpy Carpenter, Flame Carter and Shada Pfleuger (from left) pose with Capt. Ben Hindman. As "Major Oscar," Hindman kept the radar stations in perfect operating condition and insured that the WARDs plotted properly.

Above: Hawaii resident Jean Wilson proudly poses in dress uniform at a friend's home in Nuuanu Valley in February 1942.

Above right: Bette Ballentyne, Patsu Bentley and Mary Jane Tuttle (from left) enjoy the sunshine.

December 7th became fresh. One day I was dressed in my new uniform standing in front of the YWCA on Richards Street ready to be taken to Little Robert when suddenly the loud sound of the wailing sirens began. Somehow, another young WARD and I were pressed into the back seat of an officer's sedan that was parked there and the driver took off for King Street, heading out through Chinatown at high speed. Our wild drive was marked by frequent swerving action partly to avoid pedestrians scurrying out of town to cover. This driver took extraordinary chances—racing in a lurching pattern across the road as he tore out through Kalihi. Perhaps he fully expected that we would be fired upon shortly and was taking evasive action as a moving target. He probably had

been through the attack in December and also may have been given instructions to handle the car in this manner when an alarm was given. We never asked.

"I was terrified and looked at my companion. We were in uniform and we were officers, so we hurtled on in silence. The Japanese seemed far less frightening than this driver at that moment. We arrived trembling and after the alarm ended headed down across the mud."

Nancy also describes the daily experience of arriving, after somewhat less harrowing rides, at Little Robert. "At the entrance to the muddy wasteland the road was rutted and scarcely paved. The nearly incessant rain that winter created difficulties for the drivers and hazards for pedestrians. To approach the entrance of the Command Center we had to walk through very slushy terrain. We'd emerge from the rear of the truck and move as a group past an initial sentry stationed near a small building by the turnaround area. After passing this screen, we'd move in single file along a boardwalk that was roughly laid down to support the pedestrian from contact with puddles of water and deep mud that lay below. Winifred 'Bam' Sperry was noted for a belly flop into the mud and once she'd had the audacity to sound out 'Foe!' when the guard outside Robert uttered the classic challenge, 'Halt, who goes there? Friend or foe?' The sound of a retracting bolt was heard and our attention immediately sharpened by this sound. The sentry was calmed by a military person who explained that these women had been coming to the Command Center regularly. The shot was not fired, but the military officer in charge admonished the WARDs that such levity was inappropriate and dangerous.

"As we moved past the final guard at the entrance to Little Robert, we changed shifts with elaborate care. The front door was approached from a small stoop that we reached by climbing several wooden stairs. To maintain darkness an inner vestibule had been created by hanging thick Army blankets, which were usually wet. Inside was a draped area through which we moved to divest ourselves of raingear, helmets, and gas masks. As we stepped past the curtains into the operations room of Little Robert, the lighting and sense of vital interaction and focus were striking."

In the month of January, Valeria Coon Dotterrer was busily preparing the housing for the 100 WARDs who were due to move into quarters on the first of February. Val had resigned her affiliation with the Honolulu Gas Company and assumed new duties with the WARDs as dietician at the Ft. Shafter Officers' Club and Resident Supervisor of the WARDs. Her position required her to be in charge of the quarters and furniture. She did not work at all in the tunnel or become a plotter.

Dorothy "Dottie" Beach, whose picnic plans had been interrupted by the December 7th attack, heard about the WARDs through friends on Oahu. The organization already was underway when she joined, and she moved into quarters in 1942. Staff member Val Coon, whom she had met while swimming at the club, invited Dottie to live with her and they became, and still are, fast friends—"like sisters"—according to Val. Dottie recalls vividly the dress uniforms, the fatigues, wearing hats, training with pistols, and gas mask tests.

"We heard that Manila had fallen early in January and that General Douglas MacArthur had withdrawn with a promise to return," Nancy Hedemann recalls. "General Jonathan Wainwright held the fortification at Corregidor with a brave group, until his ultimate surrender on May 6, 1942. This news sent our spirits down sharply.

"Kathy Cooper, Bette Ballentyne and I had chosen to live together when we met at Iolani Palace for the first meeting of the WARD. On February 1st we moved into #360E, a two-bedroom unit, where I drew the small, single bedroom. Kathy and Bette had the larger bedroom. It seemed that we had inherited a black and white pregnant cat, which we named Isolde.

"Although these were tense times, we had many, many laughs. We were all just twenty and hysterical situations were to be found everywhere, except during our periods of active duty. Both Kathy and I had married at age nineteen and Bette had not yet been caught up in the dating frenzy that characterized the post-Midway phase of the war experience for the WARDs. So, being on the same Shift 2, we spent time together and kept company walking about the Post. This was the period of writing ditties and the commencement of the WARD bulletin, *Drawn and Quartered*.

"Our generally high spirits, similar to expressions in college life, were periodically dampened by bad news. When the cruiser *Houston* went down in the Sunda Strait in the Battle of the Java Sea between February 28 and March 1, 1942, Kathleen Lowery Hamlin learned from the Chaplain that her husband, Lt. Harold Hamlin, was missing in action. 'Kak,' as she was called, was born in Hawaii, a local girl, and had married a Naval officer prior to the outbreak of war. Evacuation was a possibility till she told authorities that she was a native of Hawaii and did not wish to leave her home. Later, word came that Hal was a prisoner of war in Java."

Jean Wilson's detailed diary records precise dates and activities. At work Jean moved

Written by Bette Ballentyne, Evanita Sumner, Elaine Shea and Ruth Sykes, "The Saga of Isolde" tells of staff member Julie Carpenter's attempt to evict their adopted pet.

```
The Saga Of Isolde, or Julie is a Meanie

Julie came around one day
And said Isolde couldn't stay,
(But I don' know why, do you?)
And through these verses you will find
We did our best to change her mind.

She said that our Isolde stunk,
And that the place was full of Junk
That she had spread around the place
She said she thought it a disgrace.

When fish nigbt came 'round we all had to save
The best of our plate for Isolde (&Nancy West) so brave,
Now Hitler became the fly in her ointment
When he left the row to keep an appointment,
She slept on the bed, the hikie, the floor
She did what she pleased and a whole lot more.

She caught the insects large and small
Had kittens winter, spring, and fall,
And never failed to catch the mouse
That dared to wander in a house.

The next tale to tell in the sad little rime
Was once when Isolde was near to her time,
A storm was raging 'twas black all around
When all of a sudden we heard a grim sound.
"Tis Isolde", we said.  So out in the rain
Unmindful of weather went Jack and Elaine
Into the bomb shelter, they fearlessly sped.
When into the darkness the poor cat had fled
And there was Isolde thin but alive,
She'd presented the world with a family of five(.

So here you have the solemn truth
From Bette, Eva, Shea, and Ruth.

Isolde, Isolde how we love you, dear Isolde
Altho you had Five litters a year
360E will 88 r hold you daar.
```

Top left: Bette Ballentyne (left) and Ruth Sykes (center) tease Elaine Shea in front of their quarters. Note the bucket of sand on the step, a precaution against the threat of incendiary bomb attacks.

Top right: Daisy Williams (left) and Margery Bailey lounge on the grass in front of the simple, two-story wood apartments that the WARDs called home.

Bottom: The WARDs enjoy a special dinner party at the Officers' Club.

from plotter to record plotter; in her free time she spent hours doing volunteer work with the Community Chest and Red Cross and at the Army piers where she served cookies and coffee to departing and arriving service men.

Jean and her roommates, Shada Pflueger Bryan and Sybil Scribner Upton, all had homes to go to during off hours, so their Ft. Shafter quarters were used mostly for sleeping. Jean and Shada often entertained the military men and WARDs at their lovely homes.

Maili Frost Yardley recalls, "As far as the WARDs went, our associations were strictly with the officers, and we were told to keep our association with enlisted men to a minimum, particularly at work. Dating was almost a full-time job, whether this involved married men or not. It did not matter which, because, as Pat Swenson said, they considered us the same ilk as their sisters, and never gave a thought to not being gentlemanly towards us." Maili also recalls, "Curfew on the post was set for 10:00 p.m. and all the visitors had to be off the post. Well, once Mary Erdman, our Supervisor, told a certain General, 'Off you go, it's now 10:00 p.m." He couldn't believe he had to go, but go he did!"

Lornahope Kulhman De Clue was a sophomore at the University of Hawaii at the time of the attack. She heard about the WARD through a letter advising her to report to Iolani Palace if interested. It was very confidential, and she was not to talk to anyone about the job. Very much wanting to help in the defense of the Islands, she joined.

Military wife Kathy Cooper also remembers her initiation into the WARD. "The harsh and cruel realities of war filled everyone's life, but we had hope and wanted to help in the struggle for victory as best we could. My father had been scheduled for new duty on the mainland before the December 7th attack, but he stayed in Pearl to direct the extensive repairs so urgently needed. In late December I bid tearful farewells to my family as they boarded a jam-packed ship travelling in convoy with several others. Although my father was very reluctant to leave me in Hawaii, I had pleaded with him so much that he finally had taken my name off his list. In a day or so, a friend called me at the home of a girlfriend with whom I was staying and asked me if I would be interested in doing important and secret work for the Army. That was exactly what I wanted, and I signed up at Iolani Palace and had a friend of my father's write me a letter of recommendation.

Joy Shaw became an informal "Ma" for the younger girls. "I learned about the WARD from the wife of the Executive Officer at the Marine Barracks," notes Joy. "She was well connected socially on the island as well as the mainland, a very colorful lady, an heiress from the beer industries of St. Louis. She had been asked to suggest names of people who might want to stay and help with the WARD. Although my family wanted me to return, my husband thought it was silly to return to the mainland since the Islands were not going to be captured and we thought it was good to be helpful in winning the war. Many friends were evacuated.

"I was with the group at its inception. I took my training with Signal Corps instructors at Iolani Palace. I had a physical and took a Civil Service Exam, and moved to Shafter. The quarters were very pleasant, basic furnishings and we added our own touches. We had special training with fire hoses, guns and air raid drills. Trenches were dug all over the place that we could crawl into in the event of an air raid. Most meals were taken at the Officers' Mess, Ft. Shafter. We often cooked evening meals in our quarters when we were all off duty at the same time. There were religious services on the base.

"I was a shift captain and President of the group for all the time I was with the WARD. Generally, the group was a happy one. The sharing of all sorts of responsibilities that we'd never known existed before WARD made for much growing up. We were delightfully aware of being a part of a most important phase in the war. The most dismal times came when one of the group lost a husband, killed or missing in action. We took it as a personal threat to all of us. Sometimes some of us became dismal when the lack of sleep, due to rapidly changing shift times, came about.

"I had thirty-six hours off every ten days. When my husband was available we would take off to a wonderful beach house on the windward side that a group of us had rented together. I rented it from one of the 'Town' WARDs. I still dream of that lovely place. We liked it best when we were alone over there, but that was rare. We did, however, have a bunch of fun when the place was full of people: rare combinations of food and cocktails, all sorts of games, and 'Ma' yelling, 'Who is going to clean up the kitchen this time?' (I had been appointed Mother Hen and overseer of sanitation and housekeeping.)

Trained and in service, the earliest members of the Women's Air Raid Defense prepared to face the uncertain days ahead. With continued U.S. defeats throughout the Pacific, the fear of another attack loomed ever present. If the Japanese came back, would they be ready? If they were ready, would it make a difference? Perhaps the early days of their experience was marked most by the irreconcilable tension between the desire to have their new skills tested and the terror that they would be.

Shada Pfleuger's playful "No Snafu" (Situation Normal-All Fouled Up) party map makes use of code names and landmarks familiar to "Rascals" and "Oscars."

Below: Margery Bailey (left) and Patsy Soost soak up the sun on R & R at Lanikai Beach.

Hawaii WARDs, bottom row, left to right: Henrietta Estes, Amy Aki Yap, unidentified, Gladys Moku Spencer, Mary Kim Yuen, Mabel Moku Obina, Mary Chee. Second row: Miss Victor, Dorothy Choy, Esther Chow, Marcella Dosall, Louise Freitas, Connie Torrijos, Ah Ngun Ah Mai. Third row: Matilda Serrao, Miss Chalmers, Mildred Fontes Williams, Bertha Herrman Paris, Dorothy Wong Branco, Harriette Kama, Sarah Kualii Chun. Fourth row: Velma Rocha, Elizabeth Decker, Violet Nathaniel, Helen Kim Young. Fifth row: Elizabeth Edmunds, Ellen Swain, Miss Carvalho, Louise Bothelo, Martha Ahuna Fisher, Betty Gibson, Virginia Haaunio.

Hawaii WARDs, bottom row, from left: Betty Chan Nelson, Nellie Palacio, Chris Palacio, Thelma Fergerstrom Teves, Florence Chong Lee, Lucy Akiona, unidentified, Hazel Bush (Unit Supervisor). Second row: Anna Choy, Chun Yen Lai, Harriette Notley, unidentified, Helani Naipo, Whilhelmina Like, Leilehua Racelis. Third row: Elizabeth Kualii Afook, Ernestine Bothelho, E. Perez, Aloha Racelis Carvalho, Irene Perez, Vivian Cambra, Oi Guan Yuen. Fourth row: Emmaline Simmons, Margaret Hohu, Lois Lee, unidentified. Fifth row: Patricia Hook, Margaret Gardner, Kahiwa Rosehill, Helen Ann Cran, Winnie Hamaku, Katherine Borden.

The military installations on Oahu had been Japan's focus during the December 7th attack—no other island in the chain had been singled out for attack. The neighbor islands of Hawaii, however, were not immune, and several incidents revealed their vulnerability to attack, a vulnerability intensified by their distance from the major military installations on Oahu. The so-called "Battle of Niihau" during which a Japanese pilot crash landed on the island of Niihau and terrorized the local population, and the shelling of Nawiliwili Harbor, Kauai and the harbor towns of Hilo, Hawaii and Kahului, Maui by Japanese submarines on December 30 and 31, 1941, brought the reality of war to neighbor island residents.

To improve the coverage of the Air Defense System, radar stations and WARD units were established on the neighbor islands. The fixed SCR-271 radar at Haleakala on Maui came on line in February 1942 and, shortly after, a unit at Kokee on Kauai. Proving further that the SCR-271 was not suited for high altitudes, their performance generally was a great disappointment. Mobile SCR-270s later were installed near the sites. On the island of Hawaii, an SCR-271 was installed at Pahoa and a mobile radar at Kahuku Ranch. As the war progressed, so did the versatility and usefulness of radar, but the backbone of the Aircraft Warning System for the islands would remain the mobile SCR-270 system.

At the request of the Honolulu command, the Maui Center was established as part of the inter-island network on July 30, 1942. WARDs Mary Louise Weller Case and Ellin White Burkland accompanied Lieutenant Colonel Cole, Army Air Corps, and two Signal Corps officers, Captain Anthony Kransus and Captain Howard Cord, to Maui to set up the Center.

Recruitment for the Maui Center was conducted primarily by word of mouth. Some of the women heard about it at their jobs, some through friends, and several claim they read it as an ad in the *Maui News*. Some of the recruits joined immediately after high school graduation.

The first supervisor was Mrs. Henrietta McCaustland, director of the Maui Girls Scouts at the time of the blitz. Mrs. McCaustland soon needed to return to the mainland, and Mrs. Amelia Lightner was hired to replace her. Alma Anton, a resident nurse, was recruited to head the dispensary, a requirement to opening a Center.

The Good Shepherd Church in Wailuku had a large recreation building and a rectory in the back of the grounds that parishioners had turned over to the military. An easily accessible location, the Church became the Maui Center, and engineers soon turned Church buildings into a plotting room and staff facilities. Sandbags and heavy planting helped camouflage the area. No one in town—not even their families—were aware of where the WARDs worked or what they did. The women were extremely careful not to reveal any clue of duty or job and were dropped off for work away from the Center so no one would see where they went.

Most of the women lived at home and had transportation to work, so living accommodations were not a particular problem. A limited number of girls, about five, housed first at the Wailuku Hotel then at the Haleakala Hotel, both located within walking distance of the Center. Mrs. Martha Gray was the Resident Supervisor, and the boarders recall that she was firm and held room inspections regularly wearing white gloves! Although they had cooking privileges, most ate out or at home. The women had fatigues like the Oahu WARDs, but they did not have the dress uniforms. They worked eight-hour shifts, with fifteen girls to a shift. They did not have a stand-by "Town Reserve" group as Honolulu did and had to manage with the regular shift.

Only the island of Maui was shown on the main, 6' by 18', plotting board, with the rest of the islands charted on an adjacent wall. Each shift included a filterer, six plotters, a record plotter, switchboard operator and teletype operator who controlled a direct line to the Naval Air Station at Puunene. All the women were trained by Sgt. Potts who had accompanied the group that established the Center. At first, visual spotters on top of Haleakala and in Wailua, East Maui, supplemented the radar unit. The visual readings, however, proved too unreliable due to the weather and were soon done away with.

Chapter Four

"Adolf, run for cover, Tojo, put away your sword! The program will be different, since the BRATS have joined the WARD."

Ode to Kauai's high school recruits

Top to bottom:
Staff Sgt. Potts and his
trusty dog. Henrietta
McCaustland and
Amelia Lightner served
as supervisors of the
Maui unit. Resident
nurse Alma Anton
headed the dispensary.

Activities in the filter center involved working closely with the Naval Air Station on Maui on intercept practice so that Lizard could be alerted to any unidentified flights. There were about 25,000 Marines and Army and Navy men on Maui, hence the WARD's social life was never wanting! A picnic, party or dance with the men from the stations always was scheduled.

The Hilo unit of the WARD on the island of Hawaii began operations on August 10, 1942 under the supervision of Mrs. Hazel Bush. Mrs. Bush began recruiting in June, 1942; soon she had approximately twenty-six women attached to the command. The officer attached to the unit was Lieutenant Balbin, who also had been on Oahu. Again Ellin White Burkland, this time assisted by Rachel Roehm, travelled to Hilo to help establish the Center. They stayed two weeks in Hilo interviewing girls and getting uniforms and the necessary paperwork underway. Mrs. Bush recalls that the office was not given any G.I. issue furniture so she had to call on her husband to get office furniture. They assembled the essentials—file cabinets, desks, chairs—from second hand stores and donations, and as Lt. Balbin noted, "It was left up to us to fetch them!"

As the Kauai unit was established at about the same time as the Hilo unit, Mrs. Bush travelled to Kauai to see their operation. Just before leaving for Kauai on an Army plane, Mrs. Bush was astonished to see the pilot studying the route to Kauai from a map drawn on the ground by another officer!

The hardest part of Mrs. Bush's job was making sure that the girls showed up for their shifts as the young officers always wanted them to go off on dates. She also recalls that some of the ladies who applied were over the age limit. When turned away, they angrily noted, "Well, you're over the limit, too!" And so she was.

The radar that was used for tracking on the island of Hawaii was located on Kahuku Ranch and at Pahoa Village. In the beginning readings from both stations were transmitted by radio.

Mrs. Florence Burton Rice was chosen to be Head Supervisor and recruiter of the Kauai unit. A more trusted and respected person could not have been found. Mrs. Rice was known throughout the Islands for her generosity and community work. She and her husband, Judge Philip Rice, were viewed as carrying on the tradition set by Philip's parents, Mr. and Mrs. William Hyde Rice. William Rice was esteemed for his good works and vast knowledge of the Hawaiian language. During his life he had accumulated an extensive collection of Hawaiian chants and folklore, much of which he could recite from memory. His wife, Mary Waterhouse Rice, had organized "Hui Aloha" (aloha group), a benevolent society composed mainly of Hawaiian women. The Hui had become a force that united and supported the Kauai community, and the group was greatly respected for helping anyone in need regardless of race, age or social standing. Mary Rice also spoke fluent Hawaiian, and she and her husband were devoted members of the Lihue Hawaiian Church. The Rice's home, in which they raised their eight children, was called "Hale Nani" (beautiful house). Over the doors of the living room, welcoming all visitors, "ALOHA" was printed in large green letters. The Rice's donated their beautiful estate to the government to be used as the Kauai Information Center and WARD base.

Mrs. Rice faced formidable problems in recruiting women for the WARD. The pineapple and sugar plantations (Koloa, Kauai became Hawaii's first sugar plantation in 1835) dominated the life and economy of Kauai, and the population of 35,000 was mostly Japanese. Chinese, Koreans, Filipinos, Hawaiians and *haoles* (Caucasians) were the minorities. Although undoubtedly Japanese girls would have been willing and able to do the work— their fathers and brothers were working long hours in the "Kiawe Corps" clearing land for the military, stringing barbed wire, digging huge holes for bomb shelters, and painting camouflage designs on cars and buildings— Mrs. Rice attempted to recruit girls of non-Japanese background, without Japanese relatives, between the ages of 20 and 34. Under the circumstances, the WARD recruiting policy was understood and accepted.

To Mrs. Rice and the three women she asked to help as supervisors, Mrs. Marjorie Peacock, Mrs. Thelma Taylor, and Mrs. Mary Crawford, it immediately became apparent that high school girls would have to be accepted to

Supervisors of the Maui WARD, bottom row, from left: Amelia Lightner, Principal Supervisor, and Mary Andersen. Top row: Caroline Ah Sing Wasko, Martha Gray and Susan Ing.

Left: On a trip to Hawaii to entertain American troops, comedian and actor Joe E. Brown jokes with members of the Maui WARD.

Right: Maui WARD Irmgard Waiwaiole performs hula for Army and WARD friends.

Hazel Bush, supervisor of the Hawaii unit (left), with Secretary Ah Ngun Ah Mai (center) and Assistant Supervisor Henrietta Estes in the Hilo office.

Top: Kauai Supervisors were Marjorie Peacock, Mary Crawford, Thelma Taylor and Flora Rice (from left).

Bottom: Kauai's Shift 3 on the steps of Hale Nani, bottom row, from left: Marion Whang (Shift Captain), Phyllis Dang. Second row: Dolores Henriques, Catherine Park, Marie Castillo, Pearl Waiau. Third row: Beatrice Dang, Hannah Montgomery. Fourth row: Mabel Blacksted, Keale Tom, Violet Pa, Anna Palama, Helen Henriques.

fill the quota of fifty or so girls. Mrs. Rice enlisted the aid of prominent people in the community, among them Dr. Lawrence Patterson, a physician living in Kapaa, to identify mature, outstanding students. Once supplied with lists of students, the supervisors personally asked each girl to join the WARD. The generous response of those very young girls to the demanding Army work and its confining lifestyle constitutes an intriguing aspect of the Kauai unit.

One such student was Phyllis Dang, born on Kauai of Chinese parents. Phyllis lived with her parents and several brothers and sisters on their farm home at Kalaheo. Mr. Dang kept cows on his twenty-four acres; he also worked in the Lawai cannery. Phyllis and her sister Beatrice took turns staying home from high school to help their mother who was in frail health since the birth of twin sons. One summer day in 1942, Mrs. Rice drove up to the house and asked Mrs. Dang to let Phyllis and Beatrice do important, secret work for the government. The girls, she explained, would have to leave home and live in a compound at

Lihue. Although Mrs. Dang needed her daughters very much, Judge and Mrs. Rice were held in such esteem that she felt she could not refuse. Phyllis and Beatrice felt honored to be asked "to serve their country as good Americans" and in a few days left home for the WARD compound.

Kee Soon Kim was of Korean descent. Some time in June of 1941, Mrs. Stanley Taylor stopped at the Kim's home in Kapaa, and asked Kee Soon to come into her car for a talk. Amazed that Mrs. Taylor had ever found her house since Kapaa as yet had no street names or house numbers, Kee Soon followed her to the car. Mrs. Taylor told Kee Soon that Mrs. Rice wanted her to join an organization to do vital and secret government work. Acquiring a good education was very important to Kee Soon, so she said she would, if she could finish her education. Mrs. Taylor assured her that could be arranged and the interview ended. This seemed a great opportunity to Kee Soon, for she had to travel to Lihue to attend Kauai High School and since December strict gas rationing had made getting to school a problem. Now she would be living in Lihue! The Kims, like the Dangs, were greatly honored to have their daughter work for Mrs. Rice and the government. When the recruits were given physical exams, Kee Soon discovered that she had a heart murmur. The WARD accepted her anyway.

Mary Samson and her Filipino parents lived in Kapaa. Her father had an insurance agency and her mother was a registered nurse. Both of them reacted with pleasure and pride when Mary, not yet in high school, was asked by Mrs. Rice to become a member of the WARD.

Not having the slightest idea of the work they would be doing, the girls moved into Hale Nani. The Rice's entire estate was surrounded by barbed wire and now an armed sentry stood at the gate once guarded by Hawaiian *pohaku kupua* (sacred stones). All traffic entering and leaving the compound was checked. Night and day, jeeps, reconnaissance cars and two and a half ton trucks thundered through the gate.

The avenue from the gate to the house was lined with stately royal palms that rose from banks of jasmine, purple and white

DANGS FAMILY 1944

A photo collage of the Dang family made in 1944 includes pictures of Phyllis (left) and Beatrice in their WARD uniforms.

thrumbergia, and Japanese tiger lilies. A *kamani* (laurel) tree grew by a side door. Ferns of all kinds and now, sandbags, circled the house. Several large monkey pod trees shaded the sweeping lawns and daisies grew in profusion. Judge Rice had moved into his house at Poipu and the WARD women took over Hale Nani as their dormitory. Near the main house, a small cottage that had been a fertilizer shed was converted into a seven-bed dormitory for the high school girls. It was immediately nick-named "Hale Brats" (House of Brats). Near the cottage, on the other side of the barbed wire fence, stood the sentry post. If the sentry on duty had information to pass on to the WARDs in the cottage, he simply threw a handful of rocks at the front door. Life in Hale Brats was lively and noisy.

Although large, the kitchen of the main house was used mainly for snacks, and there Mrs. Rice had installed two phones for the use of the WARDs. The girls ate their meals in a small mess hall built for them by the Army. The fare was strictly G.I. food and for many of the girls it was hard to forego their familiar rice and noodles for hominy grits, Spam and rice

pudding. The WARDs took turns setting and clearing the tables, but an enlisted man washed the dishes.

For two months the WARDs trained at Lihue Grammar School. Men from the Air and Signal Corps taught them to plot and record and to filter extraneous plots. They also were taught to vector the P-40 fighter planes stationed at Barking Sands and to intercept any unidentified flights. Since the mission of the Kauai Information Center was radar coverage and defense of the Kauai area, the radar readings were not sent to Oahu.

Because many of the Kauai WARDs were still in high school, supervisors made sure that social events were carefully chaperoned. Annie Kim (left) and Kee Soon Kim are photographed at this beach party with Army friends.

Top: Kauai WARDs and friends picnic at Poipu Beach in Koloa, Kauai just four days before the unit's disbandment. Members of the group are identified as (from left): Smithy, Johnny, Bob Olsen, Pierre Reysen, Bobby, Lillian West, Dr. Waterhouse, Virginia Costa, Liz McCoy, and Disbrow.

Bottom: A scrapbook entry captures WARDs Dolores Henriques (left) and Phyllis Dang on a beach outing.

The high school girls report that the hardest aspect of being a WARD was separation from their classmates, especially since they could not tell anyone what they were doing. They were teased and laughed at for associating with the G.I.s and some of the local gossip hinted that they were prostitutes. They wore their uniforms proudly, however, never wavering in their loyalty to Mrs. Rice and their trust in her integrity.

Mrs. Rice was strict with all the women. They had to sign in and out of the compound and give the password of the day upon entry. Curfew was 8:00 p.m., and rooms were inspected monthly. A tutor, Mr. John Crosson, was provided for the high school students. Phyllis Dang, Helen Henriques, Annie Kim, Kee Soon Kim, Katherine Lovell, Iwalani Luke, and Harriet Lum attended classes in Mrs. Ruth Smith's garage next door to the compound. Never once asking the girls about their work, Mr. Crosson taught and tutored in all the basic courses. A few years later he became principal of Kauai High School.

The actual operation of the Kauai Information Center began on September 14, 1942. The Army had converted one of the buildings on the Rice's estate into a small Information Center modelled on Ft. Shafter's. The outside was surrounded by barbed wire and sandbags; inside was a room with a plotting table map that extended many miles further to the west than the one at Ft. Shafter. Any flights headed for Kauai that could not be identified by the Army Air Corps officer-in-charge and his staff were intercepted by the Fighter Squadron stationed at Barking Sands.

The officers in charge of the Kauai Information Center were Major Arthur Kingham and Major Bascom Brooks of the Army Air Corps, Lt. Alvin Jacobson, Lt. Kean C. Farlin, Lt. Wilbur Cross and Lt. Ralph Fisher, all of the Army Signal Corps. The "Hale Brats" belonged to Shift 2 of the WARD unit, and their shift captain was Elizabeth McCoy.

Most of the Kauai WARDs had never met or associated with soldiers, but report that working with the men gave them an understanding of and respect for G.I.s and their achievements and that they received the utmost respect and help from the men. Several of the soldiers encouraged the girls to do their homework and even helped with assignments after their shifts. George Wallace, a graduate of Duke University, not only assisted Annie Kim in writing her book reports, but also shared with her the licorice whips that his mother frequently sent him from home. Wallace later became a high school principal on the mainland, and he and Annie kept in touch for several post-war years. Leonard Mondi, on duty with the Army Air Corps as a graphic artist, also took an interest in Annie's homework. Today he is a renowned artist and lives in Chicago; he recently sent Annie a print of "Christ on the Cross," one of his most famous paintings.

Pierre "Frenchie" Reysen, one of the Mess Sergeants, also became like a big brother to the girls. Frenchie came from France as a guard of the French Crown Jewels exhibited in the New York World's Fair in 1939–1940. France fell to the Germans before he could get home, so he attended Notre Dame University at South Bend. Later, he joined the Army Air Corps. The girls loved music and singing, and Frenchie had a beautiful voice. He now lives in Bitteburg, Germany and still keeps in touch with his WARD friends.

Sometimes the WARDs would go in groups to the beach for picnics, sometimes to the movies with Captain Alvin Jacobson as official chaperone, sometimes to dances given by the Signal Corps. Almost every month the WARDs went to a nearby church hall for a dance or had a party in the main house. They'd sing with the men around the piano or dance hula to Hattie Maka's *ukelele* and guitar music. In all cases the supervisors closely chaperoned the dating of the high school WARDs. In spite of the restrictions and constant supervision, the WARDs were happy with themselves and proud of their work.

The families of the girls were truly generous to the men in uniform. Often Phyllis Dang's father would pick up some of the off-duty soldiers who camped in part of his pasture and bring them to his house for Chinese noodles and other Oriental dishes. The extra milk he got from his cows he gave to the men working with Lt. Harold Davis from Peekskill, New York, stationed at Hanapepe. Frequently Mr. and Mrs. Dang invited Davis and his friends for dinner and, best of all, if Davis flew his plane over their pasture and dropped cookie tins, Phyllis would stuff them with cookies her mother baked.

A favorite pastime of the WARDs was bringing home officers and enlisted men to meet their parents and families. The girls brought the groceries for dinner and the men spent hours helping them slice, chop and cook. Talking to the girls' families meant much to their guests, and usually after dinner they played music and sang. "Praise the Lord and Pass the Ammunition" and "When the Lights Go On Again All Over the World" were songs that had special meaning for the residents of the Hawaiian Islands! They enjoyed belting out "Chattanooga Choo Choo" and "Cow Cow Boogie," but singing "White Christmas" sometimes caused the young soldiers to grow misty-eyed and homesick.

Mary Samson's parents threw a large party for several of the men from the Information Center. One of the guests, Lt. Wilbur Cross, a grandson of the Governor of Connecticut, wrote her family a greatly appreciated note of

THE HALE BRATS OF KAUAI W.A.R.D.

Harriet Lum

Annie Kim

Mary Samson

Tamie Song

Kee Soon Kim

Ode to the Hale Brats

Adolf, run for cover,
Tojo, put away your sword!
The program will be different
Since the BRATS joined the WARDs.

They put aside their glamour,
And their hearts, once soft and warm,
Are harder than a hammer
Since they donned a uniform.

"A woman is only a woman"
Is but a Kipling myth
'Cause when they're mad, those brats
Ain't to be monkeyed with.

Rommel and Hirohito
Are slowly turning tail,
'Cause the female of the species
Is deadlier than the male.

Above: Everyone affectionately referred to the Kauai high school WARDs as the "Hale Brats."

Left: In 1942 the men of Company B, 581st Signal Aircraft Warning Battalion, wrote "Ode to the Hale Brats."

thanks. Such letters were not customary procedures for the wartime troops!

On weekends, when they had a pass, the WARDs went home to wash and starch their uniforms. One night, Mrs. Frances Wong, a member of the WARD, was supposed to bring Annie and Kee Soon back to the compound, but she missed them at their Kapaa meeting place. As the night grew dark the two girls waited on the street corner; soon the total blackout enveloped them. Two M.P.s drove past and, recognizing the WARD uniforms in the faint blue beams of their headlights, asked them if they wanted a ride to the compound in Lihue. With complete trust the girls got in the jeep. The ride from Kapaa to Lihue was eerie and long, with only the pale blue headlights piercing the black night, but neither Annie or Kee Soon had the slightest fear of riding with two unknown soldiers. They arrived at the gate of the compound about 10:00 p.m., to be met by a shaken and almost frantic Mrs. Rice who had been told by Mrs. Wong that the girls were lost. In trying to find them, Mrs. Rice had called Annie's mother, so she too was upset and worried. The uproar surprised the two girls—they had felt completely safe the whole time!

The WARDs spent much time learning to cook from Chin Soon Chun, the WARD Canteen Manager who lived in Hale Brats. "Chinny" helped them bake innumerable lemon meringue pies for the birthdays of the men with whom they worked and, on occasion, she baked beautiful birthday cakes for the WARDs themselves. Many of the WARDs helped at the Lihue Salvation Army Canteen when they had afternoons or evenings off. They washed and refilled thermos jugs with coffee and wrapped doughnuts that were distributed to Army sentry posts throughout Kauai.

In June of 1943, WARDs Phyllis Dang, Annie Kim, Kee Soon Kim and Harriet Lum from Hale Brats, along with Helen Henriques, Katherine Lovell and Iwalani Luke, marched across the stage of the Royal Theatre in Lihue to receive their high school diplomas with the other members of their class. The girls wore short white dresses, and the flower lei given them by loving family and friends covered their ears. The graduates and their families laughed and cried over their achievements.

Although the WARDs were especially happy to be reunited with their classmates after the year's separation, their reunion lasted only briefly— the next morning it was work as usual in the compound.

Only one wedding took place while the Kauai WARD officially functioned. Dorothea Schimmelfenning married Sgt. William McKnight of the 581st Signal Aircraft Warning Battalion, Filter Center Platoon, on September 25, 1943. She was sixteen; he was about twenty. The WARDs not on duty were there in force to celebrate the lovely wedding.

In November and December 1943 naval and air activity increased as the U.S. captured Makin and Tarawa in the Gilbert Islands and bombarded the Marshall Islands. Kauai radar tracked the task forces as they headed southwest across the Pacific, and the excitement at the Kauai Center grew in intensity as the WARDs plotted the ships and planes participating in the attacks.

The day before a major task force left the Islands to participate in an attack, the Army put the Kauai WARDs through a gas mask drill using tear gas, and Annie Kim developed a case of hives. It was a rainy day, and so the gas sank into the ground. The next morning when the sun came out, the gas rose from the earth, irritating Annie's hives. Nevertheless, she had to stay on duty without a relief because of the frantic activity on the plotting board. Mrs. Rice grew increasingly alarmed at Annie's swollen face and tongue, and as soon as Annie's shift was over rushed her to Lihue to see Dr. Umaki. In spite of the fact that the doctor gave Annie an adrenaline shot, it took her almost a week to recover completely.

Florence Ching Richardson was a faculty member of Kauai High School between December 7th and June 1942 when the Kauai unit of the WARD was formed. "I taught English and Social Studies to sophomores, juniors and seniors," Florence explains. "Mrs. Rice, head of the WARD unit on Kauai, visited my home and consulted my parents and me. The decision to join the WARD was entirely mine and my parents supported my decision.

"My recollections of work with the WARD program are positive. At this point in time, I'm amazed that the men who worked on the post were such nice, all-American types. I cannot recall a single individual who ever stepped out of line—amazing considering there were many young, naive, teen-aged girls among the WARD recruits! This is my most outstanding memory. Also, unlike the Ft. Shafter post, the men and the women at our unit were separated by a mere 100 yards, thereby giving an aura of one big family living together.

"Probably a great deal of the credit for the above should be given to the supervisors. They were older women of responsibility in the community and exerted discipline while permitting wholesome social activities among the WARDs and the men of the Signal Aircraft Warning Battalion.

"Hale Nani had several large bedrooms to which three or four of the older WARDs were assigned by shifts. I remember having a steel Army cot. Since I was over twenty-one, I was allowed to travel back and forth to my parent's home whenever I was not on shift. The Work Center which was restricted, consisted of a large map of the Pacific area with its grid to receive radar messages transmitted to the WARDs. One side of the room supported a balcony upon which sat the male supervisors from several outposts and branches of military intelligence. On the opposite wall was a map

similar to that on the floor. It showed the Pacific war area, again with a grid, upon which magnetic pawns could be positioned to show movement and location of air and naval groups, friendly as well as unfriendly. Considering that Kauai was the westernmost point of the Hawaiian group, its various radar stations and our WARD unit became a most strategic and important part of the whole military picture."

The sincere, heartwarming memories of the neighbor island WARDs demonstrate the loyalty of these young women toward their country and their willingness to sacrifice to participate in the defense of their island homes. Through such sacrifice they proved as worthy, professional and valuable an asset to the United States as their sisters on Oahu.

By 1945, almost twenty additional radar sites had been added to the coverage of Oahu, and several more to Maui, Kauai, Hawaii, and even Lanai and Molokai. Sadly, Tet did not get to see this electronic overkill first hand, for in September of 1942, he was ordered to the newly activated Air Defense Staff College at Orlando, Florida. As Major Tetley headed for the mainland on the Pan Am clipper, he knew his old friend Opana radar would be tracking the plane for almost 200 miles.

Young WARDs welcome a quick cup of coffee, a coke, a Spam sandwich or a donut at the snack bar in the tunnel as a respite from the demands of the plotting room.
Signal Corps, December 1942

Far right: On duty in the interceptor room, WARDs Patricia Warren, Betty Kadick, Marjorie Barker and Mary Brennan (from left) plot U.S. fighter squadrons sent out to intercept enemy planes.
Signal Corps, December 1942

Back on Oahu, the test of WARD skills, a test both dreaded and hoped for, came to pass. In the early morning hours of March 5, 1942, the radar station at Kokee, Kauai, picked up two Japanese flying boats approaching from the west. The planes came from Wotje in the Marshall Islands having stopped and refueled from two submarines at French Frigate Shoals in the Hawaiian chain. On a black, rainy, windy night at 12:15 a.m., Kokee Oscars tracked the aircraft as they headed toward Oahu. The radar crew notified the Air Defense Command at Ft. Shafter of the incoming planes by VHF (very high frequency) radio. Although the reception was garbled, Opana radar picked up the tracks about 20 miles east of Kauai and reported the echoes until they passed into minimum range and were too close for the radar to record. The Air Defense Command sounded an air raid alarm and vectored interceptor planes to engage the incoming flight and patrol planes to search for enemy carriers. Pearl Harbor Shipyard blacked out and shut down.

Oahu WARD Jean Fraser was the first to pick up the small group and track them through her portion of the board. Immediately there was a flurry of excitement. The WARDs jolted to attention as the Army Air Corps, Signal Corps, and Navy officers on the balcony barraged them with questions. Colonels and Generals showed up at Little Robert en masse that night. Recognizing the danger of using anti-aircraft fire with their own planes in the sky, they called off any further action.

In the black night and overcast, the Army Air Corps pursuit pilots were unable to find the big Japanese seaplanes. The Japanese had equal trouble locating Pearl Harbor through the clouds. Their mission was to survey Pearl Harbor in hopes of locating American aircraft carriers and if possible to attack them with the four 550 lb. bombs that each plane carried. The frustrated Japanese pilots dropped their bombs blindly, one group exploding off the entrance to Pearl Harbor. The other group fell on Tantalus Heights about a mile from Roosevelt High School in the Makiki section of Honolulu. The Japanese then flew southwest for the long flight back to their Marshall Island base.

The night of the Tantalus bombing WARD Betty Cornwell Hogoboom, her cousin and her cousin's two young children squeezed into a bomb shelter with their two German shepherds. While the children cried because the dogs did not have gas masks and might be killed, the grownups bemoaned the abundance of bullfrogs sharing their shelter.

"The progression of Japanese conquests included the fall of Singapore on February 15th, and we sensed that they would head toward us again very soon," recalls Nancy Hedemann. "The rains persisted and by the first of March I had come down with a strep throat that kept me off work on the night of March 4th and into the 5th. At about 1:30 a.m. on the 5th, I was aroused by knocks on the door by supervisors. We had to go to the air raid shelter because of an imminent raid, they said. Struggling out into the rain with my helmet on and carrying the gas mask, I heard the loud siren in Ft. Shafter as I padded across the road. The shelter was a deep trench with a partial cover and the floor was covered with four to six inches of rain water.

"No sooner had we struggled to a sitting position in the crowded quarters than two very loud explosions in quick succession were heard over by Makiki Heights and lower Tantalus. It was shortly after 2:00 a.m. Good Heavens! What was that? Was there more to come? Soon the 'all clear' was heard, and we trudged back to quarters to talk and then sleep."

Kathy Cooper has similar recollections of the attack. "We were awakened by the undulating wail of the siren and quickly dressed in whatever was handy, grabbed our gas masks and helmets, and went out into the driving

Chapter Five

"I thought 'Little Robert' a charming name, in keeping with its deceptive air of friendliness and informality as boots clunked on the wood floors."

Navy wife
Nancy West Wild

WARD Nancy West is instructed in the use of a gas mask by a Chemical Corps officer in early 1942.

Responding to readings conveyed over the headset by a radar operator, a young WARD on duty at "Lizard" uses her rake to change the position of the standard identifying a plane over Oahu. Seated above, two record plotters record each flight phoned in.

Signal Corps

rain to the air raid shelter that was across the street from our set of quarters. About twenty of us huddled in the mud-filled wooden structure that had started to slip down the hill on which it was built and had large planks sticking out into space where the boards had separated. We were all calm and joked quite a bit about my illegal cat that had several premature kittens in the shelter. We also were listening to try to hear anything similar to the December 7th explosions, but we could not. At around 2:30 a.m. the all clear was sounded, and we slopped back to our quarters, tired but relieved.

"Later we heard from WARDs who had been on duty at Little Robert how they had put on their helmets and plotted in the enemy planes with their gas masks beside their chairs. There was much confusion, they said, when our pursuit planes were sent up to intercept the two enemy planes. Not being equipped for night operations, our planes could not properly intercept, and since they were in the air, the Anti-Aircraft Artillery had to hold its fire.

"To erase the possibility of an island-wide panic reaction, the Air Defense Command decided not to sound an island-wide Air Raid Warning. Only four bombs were dropped, some of which landed behind Roosevelt High School on Tantalus. Several days later, a friend of Bud's and mine who was in Naval Intelligence, told me that shortly after the March 5th bombings, headlines in Tokyo newspapers claimed that Pearl Harbor had again been devastated by Japanese naval planes."

The evidence was there that the Japanese still could launch planes against Hawaii, yet there was also the confidence that these planes would be successfully detected. (In fact, the Japanese made five undetected overflights of Pearl Harbor using a small submarine-launched floatplane. These flights remained undetected primarily because they approached Oahu at wave-top level and climbed only after reaching the island. The flights remained unknown to the Americans until after the war.) The failure of pursuit pilots to engage the attackers on March 5th, however, was unsatisfying. Some wondered about the system's ability to go beyond successful detection and tracking and into successful interception. The WARDs, however, felt sure of themselves. Their success in plotting and vectoring in on the enemy planes had proved the value of their training and skills.

After the March 5th attack, the U.S. military began the build-up and preparation that led to the Battle of Midway, and this was the most consistently intense time for the WARDs. Hannah McIntyre Jeffrey will never forget the numerous air raid alarms. "For some reason, many of the alarms were late at night. Usually those ladies that were not at work were in their quarters asleep and so we all had to get up and go to our nearest bomb shelter. The shelters were always muddy, full of cats or *bufos* (bullfrogs) or mosquitos! It was often raining, so when an alarm went off one night I was dragged to the shelter under much protest. We had to carry our helmets, gas masks, boots and a coat. A lot of hassle—many of us simply did not want to go out in the wet night."

As a plotter, then record plotter, Jean Wilson recalls tracking numerous unknown flights. Thus she knows that many of the air raids they endured were the result of American pilots not identifying themselves properly. Jean records daily activities, such as taking litter-bearing classes, along with more notable moments in her diary. January 18, 1942: "While on duty at 11:45 a.m., a submarine was reported sunk 100 miles off Mokapu." April 29, 1942: "I was interviewed by the FBI."

Val Coon and Dottie Dutton won't forget a certain party at the Kaneohe Naval Air Station. Dottie had driven her car because she had to be back on base by 1:00 a.m. to report for her shift. Complications arose, however, when she and Val tried to leave the house. The host didn't want them to go and had the sentry stop them when they tried to pass through the gate. Resourcefully, the two WARDs returned to the quarters, excused themselves for a minute, then jumped back in the car and disguised themselves as an officer at the wheel and one asleep in the back seat. They got through the gate, only to have car trouble on the Pali. Several Army trucks later (the men helped them along to different locations in town) they were left at last at the gate of Ft. Shafter to walk to the tunnel. They were reprimanded for being late.

That spring several WARDs enlisted for shooting practice. "In the spring of 1942, Joy's husband, Major Sam Shaw, arranged for some of the Marines stationed at the Pearl Harbor Barracks to teach WARDs who wanted to learn how to shoot a .45 caliber pistol," reminisces Kathy Cooper. "I quickly signed up for the lessons. In an area above the last set of WARD quarters, at the base of the hill that was an off-shoot of the Koolau mountain range, hay bales were arranged so that our practice bullets would lodge in them.

"Our first learning session was attended by only ten or so WARDs. Sam, smiling and jovial, introduced us to the Marine Sergeant who was instructing. First, the Sergeant showed us the .45 and explained its various parts and functions. I remember I was shocked at the size and heaviness of the gun. In the opening demonstration, the Marine hit the bull's-eye every time. Not so the WARDs, except Joy Shaw who was an expert shot. I remember my hand shook constantly so getting the bull's-eye in the sight was almost impossible. Once I so completely missed the target that the .45 bullet ricocheted off the rocky hillside and hit me in the leg! Only a tiny bruise resulted but to this day I have kept that .45 bullet with the large dent in its side. We later heard that Bette Isenberg, practicing with another shift, had been bowled over backwards the first time she fired her .45.

"The lessons proceeded very well for several weeks and the WARDs who stayed with the course were invited to participate in a match. We happily agreed and the afternoon of the match we were driven in a small bus to Iolani Barracks in Honolulu. The competition was held in the basement. The walls were painted white, and black bars covered the small windows high up on the walls. Bald ceiling bulbs furnished the lighting. Targets were lined along one side of the room. The details of the match are no longer in my memory, except that the WARD team was the big loser. I personally had such a shaky hand that my shots rarely came near the target. On the way back our Marine coaches looked really dejected, and it flashed into my mind that they had probably bet their meager monthly pay check on us. I felt sorry and depressed for several days."

This Signal Corps photo, used in the campaign to recruit mainland WARDs, captures the importance of the daily mail. From left: Mary Bullard, Evanita Sumner, Bette Ballentyne, Elaine Shea.

Jean Fraser also remembers the pistol training; she had, and still has, a neat little Colt .25 that she kept with her. Because she had a tough time acclimating to sleeping during the day, Jean's most dismal times were the night shifts. She would try to sleep from 7:00 to 11:00 p.m., then get up and bathe and work from midnight to 8:00 a.m. Though the shift lasted only four days, like most WARDs she was really "dragged out" the first day off. Jean recalls how depressing she found it to follow the ships and planes out knowing that some of the husbands of the Navy and Air Corps wives were in the group.

"Sometimes you could tell when these were routine missions, but girls realized that battles were upcoming when the fleet and planes all went out," explains Jean. "We felt very much a part of the battles in the Pacific, and the place buzzed when news came back via returnees or from things we read or knew firsthand from our work. There were many sad but brave women in the group when casualties started coming in. Marian Robles acted as a sort of housemother. Tension would rise whenever losses of ships and planes mounted. Wake Island had been captured in December 1941, and we feared for Midway. We knew if Midway fell, we'd be next! Interestingly, we paid little attention to the war in Europe. That was another war."

"That whole initial period was a period of sleep walking for me," Nell White Larson recalled. "I am a very light sleeper at best and changing shifts every four days was murder in the sleep department, as was the general noise level. If only I had had sleeping pills! I lived with delightful people throughout my stay at WARD, including Mikelle Kinnard and Cecile 'Cece' Lyon. I shared a room with Cece, since Mikelle had won the draw for the single room. For months on end after the war started Cece heard nothing from her husband, a Naval aviator. During the day Cece kept everyone's morale up; she cried only late at night, but as silently as possible so as not to disturb me. To make our apartment liveable all three of us added whatever was needed from our homes. Being military wives we had commissary and beauty parlor privileges.

"There was one shift captain that felt she knew a bit more than all the rest of us, but on

OFFICERS' MESS, FORT SHAFTER, T. H.

SUNDAY,   JANUARY 9, 1943.

LUNCHEON

SOUP   10¢

Potato Puree or Vegetable

HOT PLATE   40¢

Old Fashion Veal Stew
French Baked Potatoes
Buttered Carrots
    Bread   Butter
        Dessert   Drink

COLD PLATE   35¢

Special Fruit Plate
Pineapple, Grapefruit or Tomato Juice
    Bread   Butter
        Dessert   Drink

DESSERT

Apple, Apricot or Lemon Cream Pie, Vanilla,
    Chocolate or Strawberry Ice Cream, Sherbet

SUNDAE   5¢ EXTRA

Chocolate Sundae

DRINK

Tea or Coffee   Hot or Iced

the whole I think we got along wonderfully well. I smoked Camel cigarettes, about a pack a day. Meals at the Officers' Club were adequate, though the butter was frequently rancid. The weather was either hot or rainy.

"I lived for the times I could see my husband: one night every two weeks if we were lucky. Since he was not allowed to spend the night at Shafter and we were not supposed to occupy the quarters at Schofield as all the other wives had been evacuated, we rented an apartment in Waikiki with two other West Point classmates of my husband's and their wives. There I spent most of my free time, often going down to the beach.

"Early on I resented dances and entertainment given for the aviators, because nothing was done for the Army officers who were manning the beaches. Then it was explained to me how many pilots were being lost and how bad their morale was. After that, I went to some of the dances. I was fortunate enough to be invited to several of General Davidson's parties. We had such outstanding leaders, Mrs. Erdman and General Davidson. We could not have been in better hands.

WARD Katie Smith Huber recalls an amusing situation that caused her great embarrassment. "One evening at cocktail hour Julie was entertaining men in our quarters. I had gone to the office for toilet paper—the Army supplied a lot of the basics—and had a dozen rolls piled up in my arms. When I tried to sneak in the back door to go upstairs one guest spotted me—dragged me protesting into the living room—turned out it was Colonel James Roosevelt, the President's son, and Admiral Pat Bellinger. They thought it very funny and Roosevelt said, 'You certainly believe in being prepared!'"

Joy Shaw remembers another amusing incident. "We were at the beach house my husband and I rented from one of the Town WARDs. We noticed that the house next door was occupied, unusual as most of the houses were vacant, boarded up and securely locked. Later, some of the men aboard at the time came in to report that some *very* voluptuous ladies were on the beach sunbathing in the nude. My husband made a call to the Honolulu Police to report license numbers of the cars parked in the entrance way. The police chief reported that they were 'ladies of the evening' from some of the best houses in Honolulu and that they were on strike! Later, the ladies asked us all for cocktails; we accepted and a jolly time was had by all. We never saw them again. Another frequent beach stroller was Admiral Nimitz who had a cottage about a quarter mile up the beach," adds Joy.

"When my husband could not leave the Navy Yard, I would go to our old quarters in the Navy Yard and catch up on my sleep and wait for him to appear. Our quarters had been turned into a BOQ with four officers occupying the house. A brassiere was hung on a very prominent place on the bannister whenever there was a female aboard. This alerted the occupants to watch their language and not to go barging into rooms with closed doors. One day I went into the shower—a real antique—and after a lengthy shower and shampoo found the door securely locked. After two hours of yelling, dripping, and complete frustration, someone quietly unlocked the door. I never knew who did it, for all I know, a sentry heard me, took pity, and let me out."

Nancy West Wild, a Navy wife whose husband Bill was a pilot aboard the *USS Enterprise,* has many memories of these days. Some are of the WARD routine; others much more personal. "I thought 'Little Robert' a charming name, in keeping with its deceptive air of

WARD Katie Smith and date Lt. Ed Fain at a Ft. Shafter party.

friendliness and informality as boots clunked on the wood floors. It really was friendly, but its business was deadly serious. At Little Robert we were no longer just training.

"Upon first plugging into a station, Rascal called for a line check, 'Oscar, line check.' 'Rascal, R5 S5,' he answered, if everything was as it should be. If not, Major Oscar was alerted and he would see that the difficulty was fixed or overcome by some backup arrangement. If there was little or no activity at a station there would be periodic line checks to keep both Rascal and Oscar alert. Sometimes when we were not busy, we engaged in little personal chitchats with Oscar, although these were not well tolerated. These conversations would usually start with the question: 'Where're you from?' You could always tell when a Rascal was chatting with an Oscar by the silly, animated look on her face as she talked and looked down at her mouthpiece. She might be admonished by the controller or Major Oscar to 'Knock it off!' but sometimes such conversations would be ignored, perhaps deemed good therapy for the soldier at his lonely outpost.

"After moving into Lizard, we had our own lounge where we spent our breaks and where there was a telephone in case we should be needed for sudden activity on the board. Sometimes our break was interrupted in this way. At the end of one of the passages was a

canteen where everyone could get coffee, do-nuts and sandwiches. Beyond was darkness and bare, chiselled rock. There were frequent visitors to the Operations Room, and often our curiosity would be aroused. Who were they? Why were they here? Was something happening?

"Making our quarters attractive called forth a bit of originality. My roommate Jean Knight knew someone who knew where to get just about anything under the restrictions of war, so we were able to acquire two extra Army cots. We put these together at a ninety degree angle in a corner with the ends folded under and resting on a box. Our same 'someone' built us two box-like end tables to cover the outer exposed ends. We then found the means to give them a coat of antique white and make slip covers for the cots. During the first months of the war, the gift shops in downtown Hono-lulu and Waikiki were all going out of busi-ness, at least temporarily, for lack of imports. While shopping one day for other things Jean and I discovered one of these shops. Jean picked up a beautifully carved 'antique white' coffee table with curved ends, and I bought three carved wood statuettes. On the bottom of two of them were engraved the words 'Fatimah, Dutch East Indies.' I later gave the smaller one to Fay Stanley, my other roommate, as a going away gift. She recently returned it to me as a housewarming gift, a reminder forever. Both of us had already, as was sort of a custom, had the menu covers from our passage over on the

Matson Lines framed in bamboo. Later we also had numerous paintings of Hawaiian flow-ers framed. Upstairs we did little more than buy small accent rugs and bed spreads. All of these lent an element of beauty and warmth, and we became settled and fond of our war-time home.

"On the first of February the *Enterprise* steamed out of Pearl Harbor on a secret mis-sion. I don't remember how many days later it was that I was on duty on the graveyard shift and extremely bored until suddenly a great deal of activity erupted right in front of me. And mine was not the only busy station—two or three of us were putting out arrows as fast as we could. All of us around the board could tell that the officers on the balcony also had been jolted alert. Telephone lines suddenly became very busy. Little conferences were held; we strained to hear what was being said. Soon I was rewarded by hearing the words 'surface craft.' The *Enterprise* was coming back into port! It was only a guess, but I felt sure. Per-haps before the shift was over everyone in the room knew, I don't remember. But I do re-member my excitement; I was on tenterhooks until the end of the shift, about two hours later.

"I hurried ahead of Jean and Fay, and when I was still a ways from our quarters I could see a racy little bright-blue roadster with the spare tire on the side, the top down, in front of our block of apartments. Inside, Wilma and Genevieve, who owned the car, were wait-ing for me. They, too, were Navy wives. Both their husbands were *Enterprise* pilots but from different squadrons and both had higher ranks than Bill. They had been dispatched to give me the news because they knew where I was. Yes, the ship had come in, Bill was OK, but he had been wounded, as had been Bud, Genevieve's husband. Both were aboard the hospital ship *Solace*, anchored in Pearl Harbor not far from the 'Big E.'

"It was probably later that same day that Genevieve, a petite, attractive and very femi-nine brunette whose husband called her 'Butch,' and I drove out to the base, attracting a lot of attention on the way because of the car. After all, it *was* spring. The war seemed very far away again. After passing through the gate we drove to the soon-familiar dock where we both took the gig out to the *Solace*, big and white and still. Even after we were aboard a stillness prevailed. The deck was wide and, if my memory is correct, almost deserted as we were escorted to our husbands' rooms.

"Bud had sustained a wound to the foot, and Bill had been shot through his right shoulder muscle, the bullet leaving entry and exit holes with about three inches of flesh between. How happy we were that the wounds were not serious! It permitted us to laugh and not take the war too seriously yet a little while longer. Bill told me that the *Enterprise* had been on its first offensive engagement of the war, a bombing of the Gilbert and Marshall Islands. Although not much had been accomplished, the surprise raid had been considered a success, and the ship sailed into Pearl flying the victory flag. Their return, the first good news we'd heard since December 7th, gave all on shore reason to cheer. The boost to morale was almost more important than the mission itself.

"Both Bill and Bud were making a good recovery. The doctors had slashed Bill's wound from hole to hole making one deep wound two to three inches across. In the middle they laid pinch grafts taken from the skin on Bill's abdomen. He asked them to cut out the tiny grafts in a V-shape, for victory, followed by its signature in the dots and dashes of the Morse code. They obliged.

"It was four or five weeks before Bill was discharged from the *Solace,* and so for about a month we were able to see each other quite often. Strange to say, or even think, this interlude with Bill was not a happy one. The war had now cast its shadow upon us; both of us were painfully aware that a sorrowful good-bye was hovering in the wings. That prospect now was worrisome indeed. I didn't like the look of his wound, either. The scar tissue was extremely thin and still bright red. And Bill was subdued. His first encounter with the enemy had been anything but fun, and I felt badly because during that time I had actually been having fun. His feeling about the WARD setup was less than ecstatic, to say the least. What he saw was a group of attractive young women plunked down in the middle of a war, a scarcity of women surrounded by men looking for a good time while on leave or, with respect to the Army, on leave or not.

"We WARDs became very popular, there was no getting around that fact. Every time an Officers' Club gave a dance or a ship came into port, we were in great demand, singly or en masse. It was fun and, while I couldn't say truthfully that I hadn't enjoyed myself, I could honestly reassure Bill that I loved him and wasn't about to fall in love with anyone else, that other men meant nothing to me, that I would remain faithful and wanted to be there to see him on his leaves. (I never mentioned the parties.) I didn't realize that it would mean more to him to have me safely away from Hawaii. While he loved me and trusted me under normal circumstances, those I was in were not normal.

"Bill and I didn't have a little apartment to go to and at Ft. Shafter there were rules. No men were allowed in quarters after 10:00 p.m. so Bill never stayed overnight. One WARD was fired for violating this rule and she and her date were merely sitting on the front stoop!

Capt. Bill Williams, a fighter pilot who served as an Army liaison officer at Lizard, amused himself on breaks by producing color cartoons of wily WARDs and a lecherous Lizard. This sketch features Vierra da Rosa. Williams was an artist for Walt Disney Studios prior to the war.

VIERRA D. AND THE LIZARD

For that she had to undergo almost a court martial. I think some husbands violated this rule, however, and got away with it. Perhaps other men did also, but I never heard about them.

"Our first time together off the base was spent in a hotel room somewhere. It might have been at the Royal Hawaiian; it had been set aside for Navy personnel on leave. I don't remember. I remember only that the room was a desolate place with no lights and no food or drink. On this night we fought verbally over Bill's wanting me to go back home. I refused. Our lovemaking was unsuccessful. I seem to recall that we were on the floor, but I can't now imagine why. I cried. Neither of us slept. Bill had to go back to Pearl the next day, and he drove me out to Kailua, where someone had donated the use of a beach house to the WARD organization. A picture of me taken there that day shows the strain on my face. How much worse must it have been for Bill! I feel terribly guilty now that I did not make that night a happy one for him.

"The next time we spent together off the base was almost happy. Mary Bullard, a WARD and Navy wife, had loaned us the use of her apartment in town and it made a difference. At least we had food and lights and a certain amount of comfort. Still, we were not carefree. We were not 'home' but strangers in a strange place, and war was no longer a stranger. Since we had not been in the habit of drinking, neither of us thought to buy a bottle of wine and perhaps loosen up a bit. Wartime tension was upon us and we could not shake it.

"The day finally came for the good-bye we had been dreading. The *Enterprise* had been out on other missions, the bombing of Wake and Marcus Islands, during Bill's convalescence. Now, in mid-April, after being in port for almost a month, she was ready to go out again. She was always on the offense now, and Bill would be out there taking part. We spent the afternoon of his last day ashore in my quarters, saying little, trying to keep a good face on things, and not succeeding very well.

"And there was something that disturbed me very much. I recall it only now, as I write this, and I have never mentioned it before. Every now and then I detected a pungent, sharp smell about Bill that I could not identify.

It was not an ordinary body smell, and certainly I knew Bill to be very clean about his person. While I was distracted by it, I didn't feel that I could say to Bill: 'You smell.' So I kept quiet, but it certainly didn't help matters. I wonder now if his wound might have opened and become infected. The waiting stretched into what seemed a very long time, and I never did like long goodbyes. Finally the moment came.

"Jean drove us out to Pearl. It's with anguish now whenever I think of this, that I didn't spend those last moments alone and close with him. Why, oh why? I'll never forget seeing Bill walk away. To this day his tan fatigues, his shape and walk and the cast of his head are vivid in my mind. I had the thought, 'I wonder if this is the last time I will see him,' and brushed it aside. I was sure I would see him. By some sort of contrary reasoning—bad news and good news almost always come as a surprise—the fact that I had consciously brought up the thought that I might not, meant that not seeing him again wouldn't come to pass. So I didn't worry very long, and that was my mistake.

"Toward the end of May when I was again on duty, this time on the afternoon shift, there occurred another flurry of activity on the board, along about five or six o'clock. It occurred in the same place as before, on the approach to Pearl Harbor. The first thought that came to me was that the *Enterprise* was coming in again. I wasn't so sure this time—it was the wrong time of day—but I was excited nevertheless. At 'quittin' time' I rushed out of the Tunnel and raced down the hill. Sure enough! There was Genevieve's little blue car parked in front of my quarters. Oh joy! Upon entering my apartment I saw right away that Wilma was there too. They were standing in the middle space between the living room and the dining area. Their faces were solemn. 'Is Bill okay?' I asked. One of them, I forget which, looked at me and softly answered, 'Bill didn't make it this time.'

"It took a while for the news to sink in. I have heard that people often go into shock upon hearing such news and are unable to cry. Not I. I cried. Through my tears I asked about their husbands, Ward and Bud. They were okay so far—the *Enterprise* was still out. They had gotten the message about Bill via another ship that had come in. He had had an accident on takeoff. For a while after he crashed, Bill could be seen, his head bobbing in the sea, his parachute off. Then both he and the plane disappeared. I learned this later from Tom, Jean's husband, who had seen it all. A search was conducted, but Bill was not found. The gunner was picked up, alive, only to die later in the war. I have always believed that because Bill had time to get out of his parachute (and therefore knew that he was going to crash), with memories of Perry's agony [a close friend who had become intensely distraught when his gunner was killed] still on his mind, he so maneuvered his plane to save his gunner.

"Bill always had told me that taking off from a carrier was more dangerous than flying aboard because there is less space and time in which to maneuver if you get in trouble. Or could it have been something to do with his wound? He had flown many scouting missions, as recorded in his log book. The sudden ending of those records, on May 21, 1942, still delivers a shock to me. I stare long and hard at the vacant spaces, feeling the void, as if it could tell me something that I don't already know.

"Wilma and Genevieve stayed with me for a while, sitting on either side of me. It seemed to me then that I was in a totally black pit, with no light anywhere. I heard laughter coming from outside and felt that I would never laugh again. These two good Navy friends left shortly after Jean arrived. She thought I should not spend that night in our quarters, and arranged that I stay with a civilian friend of hers. I was past arguing. I took with me a reversible raincoat that had recently arrived as a gift from my parents. I didn't need it; it just seemed to give a little comfort. That night was a night of anguish. I kept reaching out my arm, and Bill was not there. And it was dark; the pit was real."

As Nancy lay in her darkest moment all of Hawaii's military and civilian population were preparing and tensing for a battle to come. Only leaders in the highest positions knew precisely what was coming, but it was no secret that it would be significant. The WARDs witnessed increased activity on their plotting boards. The community was asked to take extra precautions against invasion. A crucial moment in World War II, the Battle of Midway, was almost upon them.

After the death of her husband, Nancy West (left) was sent to Maui by the Army for R & R. Nancy's close friend, Jean Knight, accompanied her on the trip.

WARDs plot air and surface craft during joint Army and Navy air exercises. Signal Corps plotters work on the magnetic situation board.
Signal Corps, late 1943 or early 1944

Far right: Col. Cheney Bertholf, Adjutant General of the Hawaiian Air Force, administers oath of office to Maj. Gen. Clarence Tinker and Brig. Gen. Willis Hale, on January 22, 1942.
15th Airbase Wing Historian

In early May the Battle of the Coral Sea, our first major sea battle, took place. The action threw off Japan's timetable of conquest and ended their invasion attempt on southern New Guinea. We lost the carrier *Lexington,* but sunk a Japanese light carrier and heavily damaged one of the carriers that had attacked Hawaii. An even bigger fight now was developing around Midway.

Knowing that the battle for Midway would pose the greatest threat to the Islands since the December 7th attack, military and civilian leaders strove to increase preparedness in a territory already under martial law and enduring blackouts, air raid drills and rationing. Evacuation plans were developed and announced to civilians. The WARDs were briefed on what impact the battle would have on them and the precautions they would need to take. They were warned to be ready for the possibility of the battle spilling over into Hawaiian waters if the Americans were devastated and pursued back to Pearl.

Kathy Cooper believes that the most vivid memories for the early WARDs center around the Battle of Midway. "Early in June," she recalls, "all overnight passes were cancelled, and the litter bearers and those who had volunteered for first aid could not leave Shafter without special permission. None of the WARDs could use the phone, either. Later we learned that Mary Erdman had been told by Dr. (Major) Flickenger that WARDs were on their own to handle injuries and casualties. Helmets and gas masks had to go with us always, and some of the personnel on duty at the tunnel brought their C rations with them to work. I remember Bette Ballentyne and I laughed out loud when one of the young reserve officers, recently arrived from the mainland, showed us his food ration kit that he had dutifully brought to work—the cruelty of youth! If special flights were coming in from Midway, we frequently worked without observing our usual relief time. The Military Governor's Office requested that all women and children living in the areas between Punchbowl and Liliha Streets leave at once and stay in other sections of the city."

Nancy Oakley Hedemann has similar recollections. "In May, the buildup to confrontation with the Japanese was in progress. The Battle of the Coral Sea on May 7th and 8th thwarted the Japanese thrust to Port Moresby in New Guinea at some cost to U.S. forces, which rapidly returned to Pearl Harbor. The carrier Yorktown was repaired with great rapidity to prepare her for the big battles expected at the end of May. On May 15th, in a report in the *Honolulu Advertiser,* Lieutenant General Delos C. Emmons, the military governor of Hawaii, warned the civilian population that assaults were expected against Hawaii.

"A special alert was ordered by Major General Clarence L. Tinker, Commander of the Hawaiian Air Force. The B-17 bombers were being readied for aviation prominence in the expected action. The WARDs were informed of specific preparations being made and the behaviors and performances expected during the period of anticipated attack. One afternoon toward the end of the third week of May, the WARDs were assembled in the Recreation Room to hear Major General Tinker, Brigadier General Howard C. Davidson, and Major Ernest 'Mickey' Moore tell us of the anticipated action with the Japanese. As our military leaders, these handsome, dapper men were well respected by us and their serious messages made a deep impact. They were dressed in their 'pinks' and spoke individually, starting with General Tinker who provided general outlines of a major encounter that might bring the action to Hawaii. General Davidson said that, since there would be no assistance available to us during an attack, the WARDs would be required to stay on post and prepare with fire-fighting equipment (ladders, buckets of sand and water), practice litter-bearing and generally get ready for independent self-care. Major Moore gave us more specific directions for our preparations.

"Major Donald Flickenger, M.D., Flight Surgeon, had provided Mary Erdman with a

"The happiest time was being on shift when news came that we'd won the Battle of Midway; I never experienced greater rejoicing."

WARD
Nell White Larsen

Hawaii supervisors Henrietta Estes (left) and Hazel Bush (right) photographed with Major "Mickey" Moore.

new yellow powder medication, called Sulfanilamide [a precursor to penicillin] for use in injuries. As we prepared, news came that another WARD, Nancy West, had lost her husband. Ensign William West had crashed his SBD dive bomber on takeoff from the *Enterprise* on May 20th. Bill had drowned though his gunner was saved. When the *Enterprise* returned to Pearl Harbor a week later on the 27th, Bill's good friend, Ensign Cleo J. Dobson comforted Nancy personally before receiving the Distinguished Flying Cross from Admiral Nimitz that afternoon."

On June 3rd American scout planes detected the Japanese occupation forces 470 miles from Midway. The next morning the Japanese strike force consisting of four carriers, all veterans of the December 7th attack, was located and attacked by land-based planes from Midway. The battle was unfolding.

"By June 4th we knew the battle was on," continues Nancy, "and we stayed at Shafter three days until Mary Erdman told us that we were free to resume regular duties. She told us years later that during the last day of the Battle of Midway, General Davidson had telephoned to invite her to dinner at the Halekulani Hotel. When she reminded him that she had been instructed to remain on post, he replied, 'We've won and I want to celebrate!' Needless to say, she went out to dinner and of course cancelled all base restrictions for the WARDs."

WARD President Joy Shaw remembers that "my shift was on duty when the build up for the Battle of Midway occurred. They asked us to stay put and I gave no relief to the girls on

the board. As a matter of fact, they did not want to be relieved. The usual procedure was to relieve each plotter at least four times each shift."

"The Battle of Midway was terribly exciting," states Katie Smith Huber. "We did work well and plotted Air Force bombers—many with injured men aboard—into blacked-out airfields with voice direction through UHF (ultra-high frequency) radio contact. We received a citation for a job well done."

Lornahope Kuhlman De Clue was also on duty during that time. "My most exciting time in the WARD was receiving the radio calls and sending in the information to the board on what I later found out was the Battle of Midway. I felt I played a key part or at least was involved in what was the turning point in the battle against the Japanese and the beginning of a long series of defeats for them. I was on the board for awhile but was moved to the radio receiving station in another room with Frances Slauson. It was this station that received most of the calls on the Battle of Midway. 'Fan' and I were on the radio taking readings from that area, which we called into the board. When Fan turned the radio receiving set over to me, she remarked that the readings were getting heavy. When I went on I was frozen to the radio and couldn't leave until six hours later. The sender kept telling me that something big was going on. Fan went into the board room to find out what was going on and keep me posted. When we finally got off our shift we were bushed."

Nell White Larsen recalls, "The happiest time was being on shift when the news came in that we had won the Battle of Midway. The Air Force officers threw their hats in the air and I never experienced greater rejoicing. I plotted records from a desk above the board, so I was aware of military movements shaping up from actions on the board. The most memorable aspect of my service was the respect and admiration for American women I came to have as a result of my total war experience in Hawaii. We were so often pictured as spoiled, hysterical, and shallow. The women I came in contact with disproved all of that in spades."

Taking advantage of intercepted radio messages, the Americans positioned three carriers, the *Enterprise, Yorktown* and *Hornet* under

Admiral Spruance, to the northeast of Midway to ambush the Japanese strike force. The Americans lost the *Yorktown* after a valiant effort to save her, but the Japanese suffered a staggering defeat. The four veteran carriers *Akagi, Kaga, Hiryu* and *Soryu* were all sunk by Navy dive bombers in what has rightfully been called "The Miracle at Midway." Japanese naval aviation would never recover from this devastating lose of ships and experienced aircrew.

Kathy Cooper comments on the end of the Battle and the tensions of the times. "By June 6th, all of us WARDs, and everyone in Hawaii, knew we had won a great victory at Midway, but how great and far reaching we had no idea. Not too long after the Battle of Midway, WARDs were told that the handsome and elegant and very personable General Tinker had been lost on a flight. I never knew until recently that he was on a bomber attempting to attack Wake Island.

"In July 'Fluff Ford, on duty with our shift, plotted out the flight of her husband, headed for Midway. His bomber was lost. Fluff stayed on, as had Nancy West. Both of these young women earned our respect and, of course, we were very sympathetic. The WARD for whom I felt the most concern was Kathleen 'Kak' Hamlin, whose husband was officially listed as missing in action after the Battle of the Java Sea. He had been on the *USS Houston* when it went down. She believed he was a prisoner of war. The thought of having someone you love in the brutal hands of the Japanese seemed worse than death to me. I always worried that such a fate would happen to my husband and the rest of the crew of the *Pollack,* and the stories of Japanese atrocities that filtered out of Southeast Asia and the Philippines sickened me."

Nancy Hedemann also remembers the death of General Tinker. "No sooner had we assimilated the good news of Midway, than word came through that General Tinker had been lost on a flight to Wake on the 4th of June. He was our leader. What was he doing on a flight to Wake? It was revealed that he was on one of the four LB-30 Liberator bombers that made a raid on Wake Island. Tinker's plane fell behind the flight and was lost in clouds. His plane never returned."

With victory at Midway, tensions eased. Most WARDs felt that another attack on Hawaii was improbable at best, thus the constant feeling of peril extending from December 7, 1941 to June 1942 finally began to transform into a measure of security. The constant need for vigilance, however, did not fade, and the lack of direct threat did not put the Women's Air Raid Defense out of work. Lizard was still the center of air traffic control for the island and the WARDs a vital part of the coordination of military and civilian flights. Their accurate plots led many search and rescue flights to

Above: Ruth Sykes climbs to the roof of her quarters during firefighting drills.

Left: Chemical Corps technicians set off tear gas during a gas drill for WARDs at Ft. Shafter.

Oahu WARD Frances "Corky" McCorkle.

In September 1943 The Fighter, newspaper of the 7th Fighter Command, featured an article on the WARD written by Pat Morgan. The article was entitled, "Shuffle Board Pilots" and was illustrated by Sgt. Adrian Dinsmore.

the last recorded positions of planes that had the misfortune of going down.

After Midway Hawaii became a floating supply and training base from which America carried the war into the Pacific. The Islands were used as the training and departure center for the invasion forces that would slowly wrest one island after another from Japanese control in the long march to Tokyo, and the WARDs plotted the practice flights of the associated bomber and fighter squadrons as they trained.

With the change in situation came a change in mood and lifestyle for the WARDs. Though they couldn't be accused of becoming lax, they were able to relax a bit and many WARDs have fond memories of the days after Midway.

Betty Cornwell Hogoboom says of their new responsibilities, "I remember sending fighter planes out to contact a B-17 that had gone off course, lost its radio, and was headed southwest of the Islands, and the excitement when they were able to turn it back. We were in the Intercept Room and really involved. It was the most rewarding experience I had in the WARD."

Claire Atkins Becker remembers the day-to-day lifestyle. "I lived in 355B with great roommates, Fran 'Corky' McCorkle and

Audrey Young. Audrey was on a different shift, so she had the separate bedroom. Fran and I shared the larger one. I brought most of my belongings, of which there were not many at the time, to the house so we had a living room with all the comforts! Of course, I was pleased with my uniforms, the fatigues and the dress. I still think they were attractive. And, I was proud to wear those 'wings' over the pocket when I qualified. I still treasure the wings.

"I recall some gas attack drills we had! We were supposed to wear the gas masks, which made us look like creatures from outer space—especially with the helmets! We were instructed to go upstairs in our quarters and even stand on chairs and beds to get above the gas. It was pretty nasty smelling stuff, but we all survived the 'attack.'

"Most of us did our own hair, then we sat outside in the sunshine to dry it. I remember the Officers' Club where we ate and often danced. Artie Shaw, then a warrant officer in the Navy, and Claude Thornhill came to the club to play a couple of times. I don't know if the others had commissary privileges—all of us in 355B did because we were service wives. Fran was Marine Corps, Audrey, Army Air.

"I recall a few instances where a relief operator came into the operations room with our head of WARD, Gwendolyn Williams. Gwen then would take the poor Rascal away, and we knew what she had to say: the girl's husband had been killed. Awful!

"One interesting episode I'll never forget. Our shift captain, Kak Hamlin, was visiting us in our quarters. We were listening to Radio Tokyo and 'Rose' was giving out names and places of the captured. Hal Hamlin, who was a USNA classmate of my husband, had been on the *Houston* when it was sunk in the Java Sea. Kak received no word and feared him dead for months. We heard Rose give Hal's name as a POW in a Java prison camp. You can imagine how dramatic that was!"

Kathy Cooper will never forget the mysterious laundry snatcher. "Most of us did our laundry by hand and hung it on the lines strung across the back yards of our quarters to dry. One October morning in 1942, my roommates and I discovered that some of the laundry we had left hanging outside overnight was no longer there. Specifically, two bras and two panties were missing, but the uniforms and towels were untouched. We were annoyed but soon forgot about it, although replacements were hard to get. About a month later I left my only two-piece swim suit and a beach towel and Nancy [Hedemann] one of her expensive, custom-fitted Love bras on the line overnight. Only the towel was there in the morning.

"By now all of us were irritated and we talked to our other WARD friends about it. Most of them said things like: 'Why don't you take your laundry in at night like everybody else?' Somewhat miffed, we did as they suggested, although in our hearts we knew we had the right to leave our laundry on the line at night if we wanted to do so. In a few weeks time the crunch got to us again and the laundry spent the night on the line. Again, in the morning we discovered some panties and bras were missing.

"With a feeling of outrage, we went up to the headquarters to discuss things with Julie Carpenter, one of the staff. Julie was 'older': about thirty, perfectly groomed, her dark hair always beautifully done, her nails long and red and flawless. To me she was the epitome of sophistication. Smoking a cigarette in a long red holder, Julie listened calmly to our irate voices telling of the repeated thefts. 'I will call the FBI tomorrow,' she told us.

"The next day Julie told us the FBI could not help, and that it would be impossible to get fingerprints from the clothespins as we had hoped. Undaunted, Julie insisted on searching several of the quarters in our area and of course one of us had to go with her. I was very uncomfortable during the search—my deep feeling was that anyone who would want to wear panties and bras belonging to someone else must be a little weird. Of course we found nothing from the search, and Julie then suggested that we set a trap for the thief. By now, Bette [Ballentyne] and Nancy had managed to detach themselves from the proceedings and I was left to deal with Julie. She told me to hang out some laundry, including some bras and panties, and to sit by the backdoor after dark and wait for the thief to come. Then with my blackout flashlight blazing I would discover the culprit.

"That night, very reluctantly, I did as Julie directed. No one was home, but I could hear

sounds of talking and laughing from the other quarters. Sitting there in the dark, a peculiar and ominous fear slowly enveloped me and wild thoughts of a horror creature lurking in the night began to terrify me. I slammed and locked the door and ran upstairs to my bedroom, mad at myself for being such a coward, but too frightened to do anything but jump into bed with all my clothes on.

"The next morning everything was on the line, untouched. We lost all interest in catching whoever it was who stole our clothes. Bette and Nancy and I would, in months to come, mention the thefts and laugh about them. Julie Carpenter, undoubtedly busy with other WARD problems and decisions, never spoke, at least to us, about the whole episode.

Top: Evelyn O'Brien (left) and Kak Hamlin in front of quarters at Ft. Shafter.

Bottom: Barbara Thrall, Elsie Wolfe, Barbara Pfisterer and Elaine Carlson (from left) swim at Ft. Shafter.

This snapshot of WARDs in downtown Honolulu on the day of their departure from Hawaii show that then, as now, occasions were celebrated with an exuberance of lei exchanged. From left: Maggie Foley, unidentified, Jane Ouerbach, Flame Carter, Sandra Todd, Patsu Bentley, Ann Gordon.

Of the days after the Battle of Midway, Kathy remembers, "As the war progressed, our work became somewhat routine. I was very interested in what we were doing, though, and became a filterer. There were constant training missions and many routine flights arriving and leaving Hawaii that kept us busy. We all preferred being busy. As my husband made constant war patrols in Japanese waters, he was in and out of Hawaii: away for two months, in for three or four weeks, and out again for two months. One time the *Pollack* had a refitting at

Midway instead of returning to Pearl, so that was a long haul. I was the only *Pollack* wife here in Hawaii, however, and Bud and I were grateful that I could be here.

"Shopping was a diversion, although it could be quite frustrating because of the many shortages. Downtown we frequented Liberty House, McInerny, Carol and Mary's, and Grossman Moody but, as was true for every other business in Hawaii, their stocks were quickly depleted as soon as a shipment of clothes, shoes or household goods was put on the shelves. Most of us adjusted very well to doing without any pretense of selection or choice; we felt lucky to get a pair of shoes or a swimsuit that more or less fit. Benson Smith's Drug Store on Fort Street was a popular spot for a quick lunch or a soda while shopping.

"I particularly liked to shop at Gump's, a beautiful store in Waikiki on the corner of Lewers and Kalakaua. (The white-walled, blue tile-roofed building is still there.) Their intriguing and expensive stock was greatly diminished but every once in a while WARDs would be able to buy china or silver for wedding presents. I remember a beautiful Chinese brocade slacks suit that Bud bought for me from there once when he was in port. The original Waikiki Theatre, which we all thought so beautiful, was about a block away from Gump's. Of course, no movies could be shown at night because of the blackout regulations but in the morning and afternoon movies were packed."

Joy Shaw comments on the social atmosphere: "There were some divorces but they were not connected in any way to WARD social activities, with one exception. A handsome C.O. came aboard and fell in love with a pretty WARD—this caused one marriage and two divorces. For a while after, the nickname for WARD was 'We Are Ready Daddy.'

"The social activities for the WARD or given by WARD were delightfully proper and attended by a host of important military men and outstanding Island people. I was always properly impressed. I admit to being shocked at some of the freewheeling sexual activities I saw, and no one covered up, at some of the *other* parties we went to. (We belonged to an organization called the 'It's a Wonderful World Club,' designed for letting off steam and for-

HEADQUARTERS 7TH FIGHTER WING AAF
OFFICE OF THE COMMANDING GENERAL
APO 958

In reply refer to: 27 January 1945

MEMORANDUM:

TO   : WARD Bulletin Board

        It is desired to express my personal appreciation for the splendid cooperation and assistance rendered by those members of the WARD, who volunteered to accept "blind dates" for the 7th Fighter Wing Party, Friday evening, 26 January 1945.

        It is realized that several of these "blind dates" became somewhat of a problem before the evening was over, and I know that the overall success of the party was due largely to the cheerful and cooperative attitude of members of the WARD who, in several instances, were faced with situations of a rather unpleasant nature.

        To all members of the WARD who participated, I offer my sincere gratitude and thanks for their grand efforts in making the party a success.

                                        JOHN M. WEIKERT,
                                        Colonel, Air Corps,
                                        Commanding.

The Women's Air-Raid Defense

requests the pleasure of your presence at their

Dinner Dance

December 6, 1943   1700 'til 2130

R. S. D. P.   Fort Shafter Officers' Mess   Formal

getting frustrations. It was made up of members from all the services including the Navy Nurse Corps.) A wise old doctor told me that in wartime heightened sexual activity is not unusual; he had seen the same in World War I and had made a study of it. The doctor said: 'Consciously or not, the desire to procreate is uppermost in the minds of the participants!'"

Nancy West Wild relives the Christmas of 1942, her first Christmas following the death her husband. "My roommates Jean Knight and Fay Stanley had recently left the WARD and I was alone in our quarters. I cried a little, yet I was not unhappy. Being alone and quiet— except for music from Jean's armchair record player that she had left to me—was in short supply in those days. With some male help Jean and I had fabricated a Christmas tree out of a pole with holes drilled in it where we stuck real fir branches. We bought a string of only seven lights, but they were unusual. They were large round fluorescent bulbs, white when unlit, turning pastel colors—pink, green, yellow and peach—when lit. That was the Christmas that Bing Crosby's 'White Christmas' made its debut. I think that song is what gave me a happy Christmas. It made me homesick for snow, but at the same time brought back happy memories of home and past Christmases. Fay sent me a black lace nightgown. How like her!"

Throughout 1942 and early 1943 another change affected the WARDs, a change not unrelated to the military success of the Battle of Midway. With their homes secured and the immediate threat of renewed attack thwarted, many of the original WARDs felt they had done their part for the war effort and that it was now time to move on. Some married or left with husbands who were transferred. Some left the WARDs to return to school; some left to begin families.

"My resignation was accepted September 1942 as I had decided to return to my studies at the University," writes Lornahope De Clue. "At that time in order to get a release I had to evacuate from the Islands even though the University of Hawaii had reopened. I was ready to leave the WARDs. I felt the urgency of serving was over and the need for a better education was necessary for me to get on in life. Many of the girls I started out with were ready to leave, and my father gave me a pep talk about returning to my studies every time

Top: Bertha Bloomfield-Brown, Donna Smith, Suzanne Gould, Rita Cumming, Bette Knouse, (from left) and Kitty Coonley (standing) open Christmas presents in 1944.
Signal Corps

Bottom: Katie Smith, Bunt Slauson, Dottie Sicher and Joy Shaw perform at a party at Ft. Shafter.

The numerous bits of verse that the WARDs often dashed off to one another were indicative of their closeness and mutual affection, and Mary Erdman received dozens of these heartwarming gifts before she left for the mainland.

While you're travelling over the sea,
Off inspecting or out to tea—
In fact, most any place you may be,
Powder your nose with delicacy.
Powder your nose and think of "We".
The Staff of the W.A.R.D.

Gwen, who has to take the rap,
Be it from brainy guy or sap—
Who registers sorrow at each mishap.

Kitty, who brings her lunch to work,
Who has a vegetable sandwich quirk—
And passes them out like a soda jerk.

BBB, the new-found Aide,
For whom much dirty work is made;
She types until the shadows fade.

Thelma, whose powers of concentration
Are quite a notable Staff sensation.
Whose Banshee yowls denote elation.

Joan, the poor benighted girl,
At whom the endless questions hurl;
Who brings the mail that gives us a whirl.

Val, our mountaineering lass,
Who enters each sanctum without a pass,
But cannot control our plumbing, Alas.

Julie, who grumbles and murmurs
*   of rooming,*
Who wishes that bombs and guns
*   were booming,*
For that might set our business zooming.

These are the six that you leave behind—
A better six you could possibly find,
But a bond of affection, will always bind.

Mary had a little flock
Of WARDs who loved her so
And every time that troubles came
To Mary they would go.

They sent her to the coast one day
To see her darling daughter.
Now we hope she comes back soon
As we think she oughter!

Aloha nui, Shift 3!

Mary was a little WARD
Who kept the schedule straight;
She'd jiggle numbers all day long
To decide the four shifts' fate.

She even worked the garden,
To make the flowers grow;
And every time that things went wrong
She'd go outside and hoe.

Mary stood night duty
With what one terms economy;
She'd toe up to the General's house
And brush up on astronomy.

Now she's going to the coast
To see her Mary Lou;
The WARDs will miss their Mary
And they hope she'll miss them too.

TO A DEAR FRIEND

DEAR FRIEND, IF THESE WERE
*   PEACEFUL DAYS*
OF LAZY, LAPPING BEACHES
INSTEAD OF DAYS OF FILTER BOARDS
AND JEEPS AND KHAKI BREECHES
I WOULD YOUR NECK ENCIRCLE WITH
SWEET SCENTED FLOWER LEIS
AND WAVE A FOND ALOHA
AS IN THE OLDEN DAYS.
BUT, THOUGH I BE NOT THERE TO SHOW
FOND TEARS ON UPTURNED FACE,
I SHALL TASTE THE SALT OF SADNESS
WHEN I SEE YOUR EMPTY PLACE.
I SHALL MAINTAIN A LITTLE NOSEGAY
IN YOUR HAPPY LITTLE BOWER,
AND I SHALL PLAN TO HOSE THE LAWN
WHENE'ER I SENSE A SHOWER.
SO RETURN TO US, DEAR MARY,
BEFORE TOO VERY LONG
AND WE SHALL GREET YOU, TO A WOMAN,
WITH A GAY AND SPRIGHTLY SONG.

he came to pick me up. Weighing all the pros and cons, I finally made up my mind. Still, I couldn't understand why it was necessary for me to leave the Islands. Attack on Hawaii was no longer an issue as the United States carried its fight against Japan closer and closer to Japanese holdings in the Pacific and farther and farther from Hawaii. So again my life took another change as I moved to San Francisco. I received two wonderful letters from Thelma Umstead, senior supervisor, and Joan Leblond. But, in my desire to adjust to my life at San Francisco College for Women, I lost contact with them and so with most of the WARD activities and the changes that took place."

In early fall 1942 Mary Erdman, the first WARD supervisor, also submitted her resignation to the Signal Officer. She planned to travel to the mainland to visit her daughter, Mary Lou, who had been evacuated and was staying with her mother, and to return to the WARD in a few months. Commanding General of the Hawaiian Department, Lt. General Delos C. Emmons, suggested that Mary visit various air defense commands on the mainland to study the latest techniques. Soon he sent Mary letters of introduction for the Air Defense Wings in San Diego, Los Angeles, San Francisco and Seattle.

Unfortunately for the WARD, Mary's plans changed and upon her return to Hawaii she rejoined the Honolulu Red Cross. Mary was replaced by Catherine "Kitty" Conley, who also became a highly respected supervisor.

"My husband left for Guadalcanal in November 1942, and I left WARD in January 1943 as I was pregnant and had to return to my stateside family," recalls Nell White Larsen, a military wife. "I had physical problems and needed care so I had no choice but to be anxious to return home where people had more time."

Joy Shaw, a strong, guiding figure for the younger women, was drawn away by her husband's transfer. "I left the WARD when my husband was transferred to the mainland. We had several months together and then he went overseas again. Perhaps I should have stayed with the WARD, as in his three years absence he was in and out of Pearl a number of times. I had to sign a release with the stipulation that

Kitty Coonley (left) and Mary Erdman pose in front of the Ft. Shafter Rec Center just before Mary's departure from the WARD.

I not try to return for the duration of the war. I left with mixed emotions, as did most of us, mostly because we didn't know what our future would bring. The WARD experience made me more aware of the responsibilities of military life. I have a greater respect for the dedication and discipline that goes toward the making of successful military careers. It made me a better wife to my career officer husband."

Nancy Oakley Hedemann eventually left to begin a family. Following Midway "the war moved on and we felt safer in Hawaii. By early 1943 I had become a Town Reserve and worked the early morning shift from my home. In May I happily discovered I was pregnant and shared my news with the supervisory staff. They moved me out of the WARD with a rapidity that suggested I might have the plague. On December 8, 1943, I was delivered of a baby boy at Queen's Hospital, and soon after his arrival we had an air raid alarm. My new career as a mother had started, and I had left the WARD feeling that I had been present during the most exciting and productive phase of the operation."

These departures and changes in the role of the WARD led to new developments in the group's history. Between the evacuation of military dependents and the demand placed on the civilian community for defense workers and volunteers, there were few qualified women available to fill vacancies in the WARD. In early 1943, the decision was made to recruit additional women from the mainland and bring them by ship to Hawaii.

WARDs Tanya Widrin (left) and Mary Marlowe enjoy a ride at Ft. Shafter.

In May 1944, Bertha Bloomfield-Brown wrote about the need for new recruits and the changes made to ease recruitment in "A Brief WARD History." "As the actual presence of danger to the Islands became less evident to the average citizen," she explains, "it became increasingly difficult to recruit girls to fill vacancies. At the same time, there was a steady increase of positions for the WARD to man. Every new station or job meant one more girl for each of the four shifts. It was not long before all recruiting efforts struck rock bottom in the Islands where the employment situation was critical anyway. The age limit was dropped to seventeen to make eligible girls graduating from high school in the summer of 1942. Special shift arrangements were made so a group of University of Hawaii students could work and at the same time continue their studies. The list of Town Reserves was stretched to 25, and they worked from four to six days a week on a special day-time shift.

"Although this showed that drastic steps would have to be taken to maintain the organization, it was not until early 1943 that the way was open to recruit girls on the mainland. Colonel Lorry Tindal, 7th Fighter Command, was assigned to go to San Francisco and work with the Recruiting Officer of the Air Defense Wing through whom the recruiting was to continue. On February 16, 1943 the first thirty-four girls from the coast arrived. Thereafter a quota of from four to eight girls have come every month. These WARDs sign a year's contract with transportation furnished to and from the Islands and have the privilege of extending their contract for a longer term if so desired."

The mainland recruits remember that recruiters in San Francisco invited them to enjoy the beauty of Hawaii, a highly disproportionate ratio of males to females, and the adventure of top-secret work. The value of the work to the war effort was stressed much less than it had been when recruiting the early WARDs.

The first group of women to sail from San Francisco boarded the *USS Kenmore.* The *Kenmore* left in convoy for passage to Hawaii through rough, stormy weather on February 5, 1943 and arrived to a Hawaiian welcome on February 16, 1943. The sighting of Japanese subs was reported and the ship zig-zagged in crossing. Another vessel frequently used to

transport WARDs was the *Permanente,* a cement carrying freighter owned by Henry Kaiser that was transformed into a troop and passenger carrier during WWII. WARD Barbara Champion Veirs reports crossing aboard the *Permanente* in August 1943.

Meanwhile, even as new recruits arrived, attrition continued. In September 1943, Val Coon resigned from the WARD and returned to the mainland to join the Red Cross. In March 1943, in anticipation of joining the Women's Auxiliary Service Pilots, Dottie Beach resigned from the WARD in order to pursue her flying. Mary Alice "M.A." Woolley, a Manoa Valley girl, resigned after two years to marry a submariner whose boat was involved in rescuing downed fliers. Maili Frost resigned in May 1943 to marry Paul Yardley, who worked with Navy G-2 (intelligence) helping to break Japanese codes.

The mainland WARDs brought completely different perspectives to the organization and their experiences took a different turn than those of the women hastily trained and put to work in the frantic days following Pearl Harbor. Written while she was still a WARD, Tatiana "Tanya" Widrin Brook's account has the virtue of immediacy:

"In San Francisco two and a half years ago—it really is a 'Believe it or Not' story—while walking down Powell Street late one afternoon I met a man I hadn't seen for three years. He introduced me to Colonel Lorry Tindal of the 7th Air Force. When Colonel Tindal learned that having passed the mental aptitude and physical examinations I was on my way to the Women's Army Corps induction center to be sworn in, he informed me that he was recruiting thirty-three girls for the Women's Air Raid Defense, a branch of the 7th Fighter Command in Hawaii.

"I had never heard of the organization, so Colonel Tindal explained that due to strict censorship the WARD is kept under utmost secrecy and, as a result, is the least known of the women's uniformed services. Since January 1, 1942, local Honolulu girls had been filling the quota, but as marriages were depleting the group, it had become necessary to get replacements from the mainland. The recruiting was done so quietly that it would have been almost impossible to learn the location of

Chapter Seven

"The Captain, noting the roster with the thirty WARDs, had assumed we were a branch of the Navy and assigned us to staterooms with the officers."

Mainland recruit
Tanya Widrin Brooks

the San Francisco office other than through the 4th Fighter Command or through someone already connected with the organization. Having worked for a year as a volunteer with the Los Angeles filter center, I was extremely interested when Colonel Tindal told me that the WARDs operate a filter center and do the same type of work as the Women's Auxiliary Air Force in England. They have the responsibility of plotting and evaluating radar reports on all air and surface craft for the Hawaiian Islands area. Needless to say, I was on my way within ten days.

"On the afternoon of February 7, 1943, our group boarded a Navy transport to learn that we were the only girls sailing with two hundred Naval aviators and several hundred SeaBee's. We discovered that our presence had unnerved the Captain who, noting the roster with the thirty WARDs, had assumed we were a branch of the Navy and had assigned us to staterooms with the officers. As one can easily see, something had to be done. Consequently, we were quartered in one large room over the bakery that was so hot we were never quite sure our room wasn't part of the bakery! There was

Sandra Todd, Monnie Eastwood and Ginny Watts (from left) unpack upon arrival in Hawaii.

Below: WARDs and staff meet a new recruit.

no space to open our suitcases, and as a result of a rough sea leaking through the portholes several of us arrived with mildewed clothing in our luggage.

"The Captain deemed it necessary to have a Marine guard outside our room to see that we 'hit the deck' at 6:00 a.m. and 'hit the sack' at 10:00 p.m. A highlight of our day was trying to confuse the guard each night when he tried to count heads, legs, or whatever was visible over the sides of the bunk to determine the right number—poor fellow.

"Our constant companions were the clumsy life jackets given to us when we first boarded the ship. Three lifeboat drills a day kept us on the alert; these drills were the only thing that could bring some of the people out of their bunks.

"This was my first sea voyage of any consequence and I was extremely worried about my durability as a sailor. When I voiced my fears, Mildred Heck, a fellow WARD-to-be, assured me that it would be my own fault if I were ill as, she confidently explained, seasickness was all in one's mind. I am happy to relate that though there were a few doubtful moments, I wasn't ill at all. Mildred, on the other hand, was forced to spend most of the trip in her bunk due to active illness.

"Meriwether Fielding Lewis, one of the Naval aviators, and I organized a regurgitation pool, but with each of the survivors telling more nauseating stories than the last to try to reduce the number of survivors, it became so revolting that it became necessary to change the pool to the traditional anchor pool. Everyone guessed the minute of the hour that the anchor would be dropped, and Navy Lt. John Paulsen was the winner.

"Afternoons were delightfully lazy with everyone—that is, those who weren't sick—sitting on the deck chatting or listening to the SeaBee Band. I mean sitting on the deck literally, as there were no chairs because of the danger of shattering wood in the event of a torpedo hit.

"Sunday morning, the 14th of February, several of the girls were surprised to receive valentines from some of the boys and vice versa—no one had realized that it was Valentine's Day. Meriwether and I had a wonderful time watching the reactions of the boys and girls to the greetings as we had written them ourselves.

"There were several romances; in fact, one later became quite permanent. Lovely Leona Deutsch met young Marine Lt. Frank Kalbacher who was on his way to Johnson Island. After a very effective correspondence, he returned to Hawaii eight months later and they were married.

"The most impressive part of the trip was the Sunday morning church service. The chapel was set up in the ward room and as the ship rocked and rolled and we struggled to balance ourselves on the swaying benches, the SeaBee Chaplain, Lt. DuBois, appropriately addressed everyone in true man-to-man fashion.

"When we arrived at Pearl Harbor, we were met by some of the WARD staff members and Major General Douglass, then the Commanding General of the 7th Fighter Command, who welcomed us with delightfully scented plumeria and *pikake* [jasmine] lei. We were taken to our post—it could be described only as APO 958—where we soon learned that we were a great curiosity; every one was interested in the first group of mainland girls. After signing a number of papers for the Army files at the Recreation Center, the business and social headquarters of the WARD, we were assigned to our new homes.

"Our quarters were a very pleasant surprise, compact one and two story houses with two or three bedrooms, instead of the barracks that we expected. Four girls lived in the larger houses, with two girls on one shift and two on another to avoid constant collision. The basis of every living room was a *hikie,* a large couch usually made by putting two cots together with mattresses on top and pillows against the wall. Most of the girls were able to persuade their friends to make bookcases and chairs were issued, so it was comparatively simple to accumulate the odds and ends necessary to furnish a house. Our monthly rental ranged from $8.00 to $13.00, prorated according to salary and whether or not one had the single bedroom. That fee included maintenance.

"The following day we were fingerprinted and given Territorial passes by the Civilian Identification Bureau. The next step was to be fitted and instructed in the usage of the gas masks that had been issued to us. At that time we had to carry our gas masks everywhere, but later they were deemed unnecessary. Then we were issued liquor permits by the Territory of Hawaii; the ration was one bottle per week. Also, we were taken to the bank where they changed our currency to bills with 'Hawaii' stamped on them, as it was unlawful to have regular mainland currency in one's possession while in the Territory. That law, too, was later relaxed. We ordered our durable blue uniforms through the WARD administrative office, but were disappointed to learn that we couldn't buy our wings as one must serve three months of efficient duty to earn the privilege.

"Our training began in earnest on the third day. A miniature operations room was set up, where girls were taught all the fundamentals and practiced on the model plotting board until prepared to assume regular duties on shift as a junior plotter. We were taken to two radar stations and the technology was explained to us very thoroughly. There we learned to read the scope and to interpret what we saw; we even relayed the reports to the Filter Center. We were shown several Army and Navy training films on radar; in fact, we still see all new material on the subject. It was imperative that we were thoroughly acquainted with the principles of radar to have an understanding and appreciation of our work. After ten days we were assigned to regular six-hour shifts.

"All of Hawaii celebrates each month when the moon is full. An ex-ship mate, 'Stormy' Lewis, took me to my first party, the moonlight dance at the Ford Island Naval Air Station. It seemed peculiar to be dancing in the bright sunshine at a moonlight dance but, because of the 10:00 o'clock curfew, all parties had to start and end early. From the very beginning when we took a little boat at Pearl Harbor to Ford Island, everything about that party was exciting. I'll never forget it. The next day we attended a *luau,* or Hawaiian feast, given by the flyers at the Kahuku Army Air Base. As yet, I haven't been able to acquire a taste for *poi,* the pasty mush made from taro, though, surprisingly enough, I do enjoy the raw fish.

"And so went my first year of work and play as a WARD. My contract expired in February 1944 and, with hopes of going overseas

*Top to bottom:
A portrait from Tanya Widrin's modeling portfolio.*

Bernice Stevens (left) jokes with Tanya.

Tanya dances with Navy Lt. Jack Cullen at a party on Ford Island.

Nancy West reads a card
held by Maj. Gen.
Douglass from the 7th
Fighter Command
bidding farewell to Brig.
Gen. Ernest Moore and
wife Maxine.

with the Red Cross, I decided to return to the mainland with seven other WARDs. (Mildred Twedt, my housemate, was one.) We sailed on a Dutch ship that was serving with the United States Navy on British consignment. After spending a month on the West Coast, I decided to go to the East Coast to check with the Red Cross at its main office in Washington. To pay my expenses I worked as a Powers model during my five months stay in New York. As they were very firm about not taking anyone overseas who was under age 25, the Red Cross was disappointing. When the WARDs asked me to return I realized that I would be most useful if I returned to the fold.

"With water transportation more desperately needed than ever, this trip was decidedly less comfortable than the others. One hundred and fifty women, most of whom were seasick, shared one wash room. My only salvation was that one of the ship's officers, Lt. John McGuire, a former motion picture star, allowed me to use his fresh water shower when he was on duty.

"Lt. Col. Roger Synnes, formerly General Douglass' aide and now officer-in-charge of the WARD, was a most welcome sight when he met us on the dock. We were soon to learn that there had been many changes. Major General Willis Hale had been promoted from the 7th Air Force to a more important air post with Army Air Forces Pacific Ocean Area, and General Douglass became Commanding General of the 7th Air Force in his place. Brigadier General Ernest 'Mickey' Moore, whom we all loved, had been made Commanding General of the 7th Fighter Command. Shortly after our arrival the 7th Fighter Command moved to the forward area, so we are now part of the 7th Fighter Wing and Brigadier General John Weikert is commanding officer.

"The WARD had many new rules, such as restricting visitor hours for male guests to the hours of noon to 9:00 p.m. One major improvement was the fact that our houses no longer needed to be blacked out at night. I can recall vividly the days of early 1943 when one would turn out the lights at night, open the windows, and no sooner get to bed than the mosquitoes would start buzzing around. That meant blacking out before turning on the light for the mosquito hunt. This ceremony was normally repeated two or three times before one could think of sleeping. Such conditions existed until Waikiki was quarantined because of the dengue epidemic and it became necessary to have a mosquito control to relieve the island of this menacing nuisance.

"The WARDs were treated as service personnel, given guest courtesies at several officers' clubs such as the Halekai at Waikiki, Hooluana at Lanikai, and Coconut Island at Kaneohe Bay, and allowed military transportation to the other islands. Several WARDs were students at the University of Hawaii and were given service rates. The 7th Fighter Wing provided transportation for us along with other Wing personnel to and from school.

"Much of my spare time now is spent at the Farrington Hospital [Farrington High School converted to emergency medical use], where I help by taking case histories of the newly arrived patients, most of whom are from Okinawa and Leyte. I've organized a group of WARDs and we have the responsibility of rolling plaster bandages to be used for casts at the hospital. Ten girls go in the morning and ten in the afternoon every Monday, Wednesday and Friday. We usually find it most convenient to work at the hospital before one of our afternoon or evening shifts. Other duties include mending surgical gowns and sheets and recording case histories at the Tuesday and Thursday morning clinic. On Sundays we go to the hospital solely for the purpose of visiting the boys in the wards. When one sees the courage of these boys with missing or mangled limbs, it renews the patience that is necessary to continue the fighting.

"If the function of the WARD seems unimportant to the casual observer, it is due only to his ignorance. From the standpoint of training aircraft personnel alone, the work is invaluable. Pilots drill night and day with the operations unit until they are sent to the forward bases where their maneuvers become a productive reality. As WARDs we get a tremendous satisfaction out of the part we play in rescue work. There isn't a WARD who hasn't been, at one time or another, partly responsible for saving the life of a young airman in distress."

Mildred Heck recounts several fascinating experiences before her entry into the WARD. She was an aviator and worked as a secretary with the 4th Air Force based at Hamilton Field, California. "There's always the little story about the time I 'ballooned' my landing a bit and the instructor pulled back on the stick in our tandem Piper Cub to steady the plane. Feeling his touch on the control told me he had corrected and, thinking he'd taken charge, I 'let him have it.' After the landing he said, 'Well, that was a pretty good landing after I corrected your first bounce.' Aghast I looked at him and sputtered, 'I didn't land the plane, I

Tanya Widrin, Lt. Col. Roger Synnes and Mary Curtiss (from left) unwind at the "Dog House," a clubhouse at Ft. Shafter for the 7th Fighter Wing officers and WARDs.

Above: While a WARD, Tanya Widrin earned extra money modeling. This scene became an advertisement for Matson Lines.

Left: Because gas was tightly rationed, the WARDs often used the somewhat rundown Black Cat Cafe, which was located next to the Pearl Harbor bus stop, as a meeting place.

Mildred Twedt poses in WARD dress uniform.

WARDs, including Blackie Scharbach (center), pile into the sampan for a trip to the Lanikai Beach house.

thought you took it when you corrected me.' His pale face told me what he was thinking, so I tactfully disappeared."

Mildred also tells of a unique experience that involved her with Army Intelligence, German subversives, and the FBI. It occurred before the attack on Pearl Harbor while she was working as a secretary for the Base Adjutant, 4th Air Force, at Hamilton Field, north of San Francisco.

"As I was typing my usual memos one morning," remembers Mildred, "the Base Intelligence officer slipped into the chair beside my desk and began talking in low tones. He told me to keep typing but to listen closely. He informed me that the choral society I had just joined was a front for a German subversive group, and that our Intelligence Office needed the names of all members in the organization. One lady who was the mother of a boy I had dated a couple of times was especially active. It would be quite simple for me to continue my associations but simply report everything that was happening.

"The officer was very careful to explain to me that if any problems developed from my spying on these people, the military would have to deny knowing anything about it. He told me to think about it and he would come back later for my answer. The sound of my typewriter droned away as my thoughts whirled. The decision was 'yes' without reservation. I felt it a very special privilege to be asked to help. Before I knew it, I was being introduced to an FBI official from the San Francisco office.

He very firmly informed me again that they would have to deny knowing me if any problems ever developed. He told me to be very careful; these German subversives were pros who knew what they were doing in gathering information concerning our forces and movements, he warned.

"When my friend's mother invited many 'nice soldier boys' from our base for a musical evening the next weekend, I saw the Germans' professionalism in action. Food and girls were a strong drawing card and with flattery and graciousness the woman insisted that all soldiers sign her guest book and put down the organization to which they were assigned. How obvious! Yet they couldn't wait to accommodate the gushing hostess. By the end of the evening she probably had a very good idea of the troop strength at Hamilton Field."

Soon after, Mildred became the secretary for the choral society, a natural considering her vocation. The names the FBI needed were now in the Society's attendance books that Mildred herself maintained! A chalet in the woods above San Raphael was the center of much Society activity, and on the coffee tables were photo albums filled with personal snapshots of Eva Braun, Adolph Hitler, and his staff. German lessons during which comments were dropped from time to time about 'being ready when they come' were given once a week for a select few.

At last Mildred's reports to the FBI, signed only with her secret code number, paid off and the organization was arrested at the chalet. Many were sent to a camp outside of Denver, Colorado until the war was over. Of the aftermath Mildred relates, "One day a solitary postcard came to my address from Denver. It simply said, 'It's too bad we can't trust some people.' So, they knew. Well, that made us even. So did I!"

On December 7th Mildred transcribed top-secret flight patterns for the B-17s to be moved from Hamilton Field to Hawaii in anticipation of further attacks. While her final transcription accompanied the group from California to Hickam Air Field, her working notes were burned for security. She also transcribed Army accounts of the attack that became some of the first top-secret reports forwarded to Roosevelt detailing the attack.

After a year with the 4th Air Force Mildred heard about the WARDs in Hawaii. "A colonel had arrived from Ft. Shafter to take thirty girls to Hawaii to work in the operations of the radar tracking facilities on Oahu. I was excited and applied immediately. Although I had to drop three classifications in my Civil Service status, I knew after sitting at a desk for two years that it was the kind of experience I wanted. So, off I went to Ft. Shafter for a great stint of duty with the Women's Air Raid Defense.

"A terrible storm caused our ship to roll so violently that everyone was ordered below. It kept half of the 2000 troops and thirty girls seasick for several days, but we recovered quickly when we came into the calm waters of the Islands. What an exciting welcome we received at Pearl Harbor—hula dancers, fragrant lei and a military band. What a surprise! Assignments to our cottages at Ft. Shafter were swift and efficient with Val Coon, Tanya Widrin, Mildred Twedt and I tucked away together. Before we knew it, we were enjoying our first real *luau* with *poi*, *kalua* pig and lots of hanky-panky.

"Three sets of tennis every day and sparkling flavored pineapple that made my mouth so sore are fond memories. Working together for the safety of the Islands was a responsibility of which we can certainly be proud—it helped to allay any second sneak attack, keeping us safe and free.

"General Barney Giles, my last Commanding Officer in the 4th Air Force, had made a ten dollar bet with me that I would marry before I returned to the States. Since I had no prospects, I laughingly agreed. But the day that Twedt and I dashed to Honolulu in the *sampan* to buy a fresh *pikake* lei for Val was a turning point for me.

"At the flower counter of the Young Hotel trying to get information about shipping flowers stateside was a handsome Air Force pilot, Lt. Don Leaman, and his navigator. Twedt and I helped them understand the pidgin English of the lady behind the counter, then invited them to Val's 'Aloha Party' that was being held that evening in our cottage. Val, Supervisor of Housekeeping for the WARD, was so well known that everyone on the Post was invited. Sitting on the stairs, furniture and floor waiting for the dreaded

10:00 o'clock curfew to arrive was a swirl of people in their stocking feet. In the midst of all this commotion Don and I found each other, and we knew we wanted to know each other better.

"I was leaving the following day for the rest camp at Lanikai for a week's holiday. Since Don had to wait a week for his plane to be winterized before he could continue his delivery to Australia for the Ferry Command, he came along with me. What a delightful week we had: walking on the beach, playing paddle tennis, swimming, sunning and, of course, talking, talking, talking. We felt so right for each other that it amazed us what a short time it had been since we'd met. Nevertheless, we were in love and off we went to talk to Captain Tharp at Ft. Shafter about getting married when Don returned from Australia. Many of our WARD staff were able to attend our sweet, special wedding in the Chapel at Ft. Shafter. The 'reception' that we arranged just minutes before our wedding and the chipped dishpan we used for a punchbowl and glasses and cups borrowed from every WARD are precious

Top: Swimming and sunning at Damon Estate were popular, off duty pastimes for the WARDs.

Bottom: Evanita Sumner (left), Janet Bedford (center) and Bette Ballentyne (on cot) lounge on Lanikai Beach.

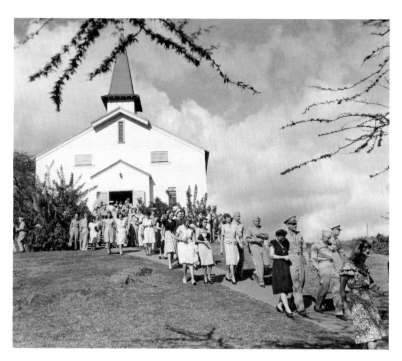

Jeanne Adler and Capt. Bill Morris were married at the Ft. Shafter chapel, as were several other WARDs. Wedding attendants are Tina Lanser and Maj. Phil Bird.

memories. I still laugh when I remember that in all the excitement no one thought to spike the punch. Reverend Tharp was really surprised when his first sip was straight fruit juice!

"Our wedding was on Labor Day, September 6, 1943, and Don left at 5:00 p.m. to report for a flight stateside. When I walked in with my crew for the evening shift that night—my wedding night—some eyebrows were raised, but it was a privilege for me to be given Don's flight out of Hickam to plot.

"Two weeks later our entire operations room was electrified by the news that a plane from the States was running low on fuel due to extreme head winds and was preparing to jettison its cargo if necessary in order to make a landing at Hickam Field. Emergency orders were given to clear the field to enable them to make a straight-in approach and a cheer went up in our board room when we were given word that the plane and crew had landed safely with their engines sputtering from lack of fuel. What a close call! It wasn't until I got off shift that I learned that my Don was the co-pilot on that plane!"

Tina Lanser tells of a particularly bizarre recruitment experience. "I was a junior at the University of California at Berkley and needed some more dough because I was a double major and it was taking me longer to get through than I'd anticipated. (My father, a very successful and very German man, felt that women shouldn't have all this education so I was on a rather restricted allowance.) In early 1943 I took a job as assistant hostess at the Clairmont Hotel in Oakland. One of my jobs was to see that the lobbies and entranceways and back halls and tables always were decorated; this I loved. The other part of my job was to see that intoxicated service men didn't cause any trouble in the lobbies. One time a young officer was being terribly noisy in the lounge, very pleasant but noisy. As I didn't feel I could handle him alone, I got someone to help me get him back into a little room where we did all the flower arranging. In an extremely drunken manner he asked, 'What are you doing in a job like this? I know how you can have more fun, make more money, and help the war effort.' He kept saying, 'Yeah, this is where you ought to go,' and mentioning a building in San Francisco. I had a feeling he was talking out of turn so I gave him more coffee and said, 'You'd better not talk this way.'

"He had made it all sound so interesting—so cloak-and-dagger—that on my day off I decided to go to that building. No sooner did I step inside when two armed guards, one from each side, closed my escape and said, 'What are you doing here? This building is off limits to all people.' Of course, I couldn't tell him what I was doing there because I didn't know! 'Oh, dear,' I said, 'I really don't know.

Somebody told me that I should come here.' I must have sounded so stupid!

"One of the guards said, 'You may not leave. Where do you live?' After I told him he said curtly, 'You will come with me. No one leaves this building without permission.' He didn't touch me but was quite gruff. 'Oh my gosh, what have I gotten into?' I thought; then I was scared. He took me upstairs into a hall-way—it was very military—and into a large room that was stripped of everything but benches and obviously was a waiting room. I sat down thinking, 'My God, how do I get out of this? I'll never convince them that I'm not up to some skullduggery!'

"A few minutes later a man came out. He was scowling and unpleasant and sat down beside me. 'God, I hate the Army!' he said. 'This darn war—we have no business being in it! We should just let Hitler do what he wants.' He seemed so distraught.

"'We *have* to stop them! We *can't* let this go on!' I argued and gave him some of my thoughts.

"Finally, he stood up and said, 'I apologize. I wanted to find out what your attitude about the war was. Will you come with me?' He was suddenly very civil and introduced himself. He took me into another bare, stripped-down military office and introduced me to another man. They asked me all kinds of questions: Who was I? Where was I from? What was I studying? What was I doing here? I told them about the intoxicated officer, but did not reveal his name. They said, 'Oh, yes. We know him.' Obviously, the man was a plant and worked for them. They were recruiting for heaven knows what. It was too set-up, and already I was suspicious."

Tina gave her name and address and was told that she would hear from them. Later that spring a friend at college asked in alarm, "What have you done?" and explained that the FBI had been going around asking all kinds of questions about Tina. Tina said they must have her confused with someone else and let it go at that. Mysterious written messages appeared at unexpected intervals and instructed her to report here and there for emotional and mathematical tests and physicals. At the end of the semester she took her finals and went home to Arizona for the summer.

While she was home Tina's father received a telephone call instructing her to report to San Francisco in forty-eight hours. At first he angrily refused to let her go saying, "They are not going to take my little girl! I'll go to the top!" Finally, after Tina explained that she would be in good hands but could say no more being bound by secrecy, he relented. When she boarded a ship in Seattle, she still had not been told by whom she had been recruited or even her precise destination.

Jean MacKellar had graduated from Stanford in 1943 and was working at the personnel office of the Presidio, where applications for the WARDs were being handled. "I was tired of being cold," writes Jean. "As I shivered in the fog I thought about what I told young women in my recruiting work for the WARD: 'Hawaii is so beautiful, so warm; the work is vital to our security; there are thousands of men to every woman.' I was fresh out of a romance with no immediate prospects. Thousands of men to every woman? Sunny? Warm? Hawaii seemed to offer several solutions in one!

"The following day I informed my boss that I was signing up to sail with the next batch of WARDs, scheduled to leave on January 9, 1944. I fingerprinted myself, signed my oath, took a physical, and processed my own application form. Then I went out and bought a year's supply of rayon slips, panties and stockings, all things that the information sheet said were in short supply in the Islands. Toothpaste, cigarettes and alcohol, it assured recruits, were not in short supply."

Dining at Honolulu's popular Outrigger Canoe Club are, from left: William Hershey, Tina Lanser, William Livingston, Tish Heberling, Gordon Livingston, Ruth Montgomery, Robert Stack and Tanya Widrin. Ruth and Gordon later married.

Oahu WARDs, bottom row, from left: Mildred Twedt, Barbara Bailiff, Ruth Montgomery, Elsa Gerrells, Barbara Price (partly hidden). Back row: Phyllis McArthur, Tina Lanser, Janie Schmidt, Geneva Bartlett, Louisiana Abbott, Isabel Vanderkloot, Tanya Widrin, Annette Freed.

Jean writes of her first impression upon arriving in Hawaii. "I was astonished to see that the Japanese in Hawaii were a trusted segment of the population—the Japanese in California had been incarcerated. This was a great lesson to me and the beginning of my *real* racial tolerance and of a skepticism toward politics and political moves."

Elsa "Sherry" Cole was working in San Francisco as Secretary to Major Brunner, 4th Air Force, when she heard about the WARD from another secretary. Both women signed up. Sherry and two roommates aboard ship came down with the flu and her first two weeks in Hawaii were spent as a patient of Dr. Kleinfeld. "After recovering from the flu, I was assigned quarters with two other girls in a cottage on Ft. Shafter. I remember that the polished cement floor had an unusual and attractive etched design of a Hawaiian fisherman casting his net. This delighted me. At about that time, I had one very small glass of sherry at a party and felt the effect of that small amount of alcohol (remember—a convalescent!) to the extent that the other girls promptly gave me the nickname I still have: Sherry. Evidently, it made me very happy!

"The pattern of hours we worked at Lizard—I think it was two morning shifts, two afternoon shifts, two night shifts, two graveyard shifts—was a real pleasure to me. I was young enough to adapt and enjoy the variety. Though older than many of the others, I was

still too young emotionally to know how to deal with the situation of living on a base with hundreds of men and only a few girls. It was disturbing to know our quarters were patrolled by military guards twenty-four hours a day.

"The happiest times I remember are two. One—the first time I rode over the Pali on the way to convalesce at Lanikai. For some reason the trip, and the view from the Pali, gave me an overwhelming feeling of joy, of something good about to happen. The second rush of happiness was one Christmas Eve. I was at a friend's house on windward Oahu with a group. It was a house party, and we'd just gone swimming in the ocean at about 1:30 a.m. It was warm and wonderful, and I was with the man I later married. I remember suddenly thinking, 'I will never be lonely again!'"

Sherry recalls some other aspects of the WARD lifestyle. "One very youthful, tall, slim girl was much involved with an enlisted man known as the base 'big-time operator.' She'd go around begging us girls to let her have our liquor ration cards so she could give them to him. No doubt he used them very profitably. Phyllis 'Torchy' McArthur, so named because of her flaming red hair, used to give us expert haircuts. One of my first roommates, Toni Townsend—a very cute, clever, witty girl— fell hard for Captain Ben Hindman, and I believe they got married. She's the one who decided to call me 'Sherry' after I got zigzag on one small libation."

Mary Jane Tuttle, another of the so-called "Mainland Recruits," was actually an Oahu resident trapped by the war's start on the mainland while attending college. Her father heard from WARD Evanita Sumner about the possibility of Mary Jane joining the WARD through the San Francisco office. Mary Jane was in the first group of WARDs who came across on the Kenmore. Local girl Margot Kellett McCormick shared the same experience and arrived in July aboard the *Permanente*.

Recognizing the need for additional hands and eyes, the hard-working WARDs accepted this influx of strangers. Resident Supervisor Val Coon so enjoyed her mainland roommates—Tanya Widrin, Mildred Twedt and Mildred Leaman—as well as local-girl Dottie Montague, that she kept in touch with all them through the years and has numerous photos in a scrapbook. Dottie agreed, saying, "We had a wonderful relationship, and I felt fortunate to have been asked to share Val's quarters. We are like sisters today. We really had a very good time, although I was a bit jealous of Tanya, as everywhere she went, the men followed. She was a dark, beautiful girl, a Hollywood starlet with a colorful personality. We'd have a party and all the men would be drawn to her like bees to honey. The rest of us would feel left out, and with good reason: we *were* left out! The same thing would happen at a dance; the men would line up behind Tanya and keep tagging. Finally, because we all liked her, it got to be a joke. She was really a very nice person."

Remembers Maili Frost, "When the mainland girls arrived in February 1943, they were accepted into the Island activities and blended easily, probably because we were all the same ilk. Military wives, being wives, were not included in as many of our activities." Mary Alice Woolley's recollection, on the other hand, is that the mainland girls "kept some distance between themselves and us local girls."

Regardless of any ensuing interpersonal relationships, the recruitment of women from the mainland was extremely beneficial for the WARD. Following their arrival, for the first time in its history, the WARD had sufficient personnel to adequately take care of operational requirements. WARDs numbered 143, including the office staff and janitresses. Of these, 136 were plotters, which allowed for an average of 33 girls on each of the four shifts and included four rotating filterers who were not attached to any one shift.

The need for the Women's Air Raid Defense persisted, and the now disparate group of women worked together to help maintain the security of the Hawaiian Islands until the end of the war. The time passed quickly for the women, and they very nearly were unprepared for the end of the WARD story.

Ruth Sykes and Maili Frost set out for "town" in Maili's convertible.

*WARDs Lucille Thorpe
(left) of Grand Island,
Nebraska and Toni
Townsend of Sycamore,
Illinois relax before
boarding the* Monterey
on October 13, 1945.
Signal Corps

The increased naval and air activity involved in the capture by the U.S. of Makin and Tarawa in the Gilbert Islands in November 1943, and the bombing of the Marshall Islands in December, caused an uproar of excitement and intensity at the Kauai Information Center as WARDs plotted the ships and planes participating in the attacks. The greatly increased tempo of work in the last weeks of 1943, however, heralded the final days of the Kauai WARD. As each successive American victory drove the threat of Japanese attack further and further away and radar coverage from Oahu increased, Information Centers on the neighbor islands were no longer necessary. On January 15, 1944, the Kauai WARD was disbanded by order of the Army.

Living under the strict supervision of the Kauai WARD had enabled the young, naive "Hale Brats" to establish lasting relationships with each other and the men and women with whom they worked. Sharing both sad times and laughter, listening to and respecting the needs of others—even eating previously unknown foods in the mess hall—contributed to an increased appreciation of lifestyles and cultures different from their own. As the Kauai of their childhood faded forever under the impact of World War II, the Hale Brats saw their world expand far beyond the shores of their beautiful island home.

Kauai WARD Harriet Lum journeyed to the mainland to join the Women's Army Corps. During her tours of duty she met her husband, then an Army lieutenant. They retired in Indianapolis. Mary Samson, always with the desire to become a teacher, graduated from Roosevelt High School in Honolulu and the University of Hawaii. She did post-graduate work in California universities and taught school for twenty-seven years. In 1950, she met and married Ed Hendrickson, a tall blonde mainlander from Washington. They traveled extensively, and still visit some of the men whom she met in the WARD. She remembers her WARD days with affection and pride.

Phyllis Dang graduated from commercial school. For years she worked at Ft. Shafter for Colonel Seth in G-3. In 1951, she married a Chinese man, and they had three sons and a daughter. Phyllis later worked as a teacher's aide in a Pearl City pre-school. Phyllis believes that her WARD experiences made her realize the value of our Armed Services. Given the same circumstances, she says without hesitation, she would proudly become a WARD again.

After traveling across the United States and renewing old WARD friendships, Tamie Song married Garland Roberts, who was serving in the Army. They settled in Virginia to raise their family. Chin Soon Chun of cooking fame met and married William Miles from Mississippi. They opened a very successful restaurant in Florida called "Hale Kau-Kau" (House of Food).

Annie Kim married and spent twenty years living in Omaha, Philadelphia and New Orleans. Annie taught vocational education with a rehabilitation organization and also worked as personnel director and executive secretary for a clinical laboratory. She is now semi-retired. Kee Soon Kim remembers her years in the WARD as happy and is proud to have helped her country. She went to work for the Federal Government, then joined an international airline. She later married and continued to hold various positions with the airlines through the years. Today she works as a ticketing agent.

Harold Davis, who so enjoyed the cookies that Phyllis Dang's mother baked for him, is now a retired Colonel and works as a system applications scientist for Planning Research Corporation in Virginia. He and his wife came to Hawaii recently and took Phyllis and her husband to dinner at the Hale Koa. The Davis' made a visit to Kauai where everything that Harold remembered, except for the Dang's house (now occupied by Phyllis' twin brothers), had changed beyond recognition.

The Maui WARD under Mrs. Gordon Lightner was disbanded on April 1, 1944. In recent years, eleven of the Maui WARDs met with Bette Ballentyne, Kathy Cooper, Nancy Hedemann and Pat Swensen. All eleven agreed that it was a job they would not have missed; serving and doing their part for the country made any sacrifices worthwhile.

The Hilo WARDs also were disbanded on the first of April. Mrs. Hazel Bush, Supervisor of the Hilo unit, recently wrote of the war years, "Those were tense and, in some respects,

Chapter Eight

"Those were tense and, in some respects, confusing times, but all in all I believe history will accord us a passing grade!"

Hawaii Unit Supervisor
Hazel Bush

Kauai's Shift 2 poses at a disbandment ceremony held on January 15, 1944 at Hale Nani. Some WARDs hold their Certificate of Service and a photograph of their supervisors. Bottom row, from left: Mabel Ahuna, Virginia Costa, Carolyn Rapozo, Annie Lum, Doris Pai. Second row: Tamie Song, Mary Samson, Elizabeth McCoy. Top row: Lillian West, Kee Soon Kim, Annie Kim, Florence Ching.

confusing times, but all in all I believe history will accord us a passing grade!" Praise does come from Brigadier General Robert Douglass. In a letter to Mrs. Bush dated March 31, 1944 Douglass writes, "This is to commend you for the excellent work you have done to assist in organizing and operating the Women's Air Raid Defense Sub Detachment, Hawaii, of the 7th Fighter Command. You were with the organization from its inception and helped recruit and train the operators. Your tact and organizing ability did much towards making the WARD Detachment an efficient, smooth running unit. By your unselfish service you have made a great contribution to the National Defense."

Praise for the Oahu WARD came from Brigadier General Howard Davidson. In May 1945 Davidson, who had been reassigned by this time, sent a hand-written letter to Chief Supervisor Kitty Coonley in response to an editorial in the *Honolulu Advertiser* praising the WARDs for their service. Davidson's words illustrate the general belief that the war was nearly over and reflect upon the historic stature of the WARDs' work. He told Kitty:

"I have seen many fighter controls, have several under me now, but the one in Honolulu manned by the WARDs is the best I have seen. I understand the war has moved on and left Honolulu behind. That is as it should be, but you and your girls can take great pride in the fact that while it did threaten Hawaii you maintained the best Air Raid Defense system in the world. My best to you and any of the old girls remaining."

According to Brigadier General John Weikert, the primary reason for inactivation of the Women's Air Raid Defense was the anticipated availability of military personnel to man all necessary installations. Weikert notified remaining active-duty WARDs of disbandment procedures in a letter dated August 11, 1945: "It is expected that military personnel will take over all WARD duties within fifteen (15) days after V-J Day and that the WARD as an organization will be completely disbanded within twenty (20) days after V-J Day."

"In view of the foregoing," continues the Brigadier General, "it is requested that each employee complete the attached questionnaire and return same to WARD Headquarters not later than 1000, 13 August 1945. This questionnaire is self-explanatory and will be used to determine how many employees desire to take other positions in the Territory, and how many desire to return to the mainland for separation from position. Advance information indicates that almost all employees desiring to remain in the Territory can be placed in other War Department positions commensurate with present grades and ability. The balance, or those who desire to return to the mainland, will probably remain on the WARD payroll until such time as transportation is available... In short, each employee will be given maximum consideration with individual desires, and each employee may rest assured that all provisions of the WARD contract will be fulfilled by the War Department."

Noting that those WARDs desiring to remain in the Hawaii in order to transfer to another War Department activity would be transferred to a new job without loss of grade, pay or time and be given a "Special" efficiency rating, Weikert closes his communique with praise. "I am personally extremely grateful for your past cooperation in all matters, and

Maui WARDs, bottom row, from left: Bernadette Vierra, Myra Dang, Florence Tavares, Agnes Meyers, Catherine Kanekoa, Margaret Nobriga, Myra Pali. Top row: Agnes Ah Choy, Katherine Choo, Marjorie Goo, Irene Johnson, Christine Kong, Nancy Bak, Imogene Rose.

sincerely hope that these necessary changes will provide profitable and beneficial results for you as an individual. You are to be congratulated on a splendid performance and devotion to duty while employed by the WARD." Lastly he adds a note of caution, "It is earnestly requested that you do everything possible to maintain your high standards of performance until officially notified that you are released from duty as a WARD."

And then, a few short days later, it really was over. Hostilities with Japan ceased August 15, 1945. The surrender was officially signed aboard the *USS Missouri* on September 2, 1945.

Kitty Coonley was in Chicago with her husband when she received these comments in writing from Brigadier General Weikert on November 15, 1945. "Many changes have taken place in the 7th Fighter Wing since your departure from the Islands. Soon after V-J Day, the WARD organization was disbanded. We had approximately 165 WARDs at that time. Eighty-seven of them returned to the mainland and the remaining number secured employment and stayed here in Hawaii. Of those that remained, five are now doing office work with the Wing.

"We wrote each WARD a letter and enclosed four pictures, two of which were from the party they gave you at Hickam and two of which were typical shots of their leaving the WARD area. I have gotten several replies from the WARDs stating how happy they were to receive the snapshots."

Weikert ends his letter by paying a high compliment to Kitty. "Again I wish to express my deepest appreciation for everything you did for the 7th Fighter Wing as Supervisor of the WARDs. Your cooperation and untiring devotion to duty contributed beyond measure to the success of the Air Defense Control Center."

For the local girls who remained in Hawaii, the war's end meant a return to their families and homes, the beginning of families of their own, the resumption of their educations. They would never return, however, to their pre-war lifestyles. World War II had changed Hawaii dramatically and permanently. Development and urbanization began immediately; high rises sprung up. Cheap and easy air travel suddenly brought unprecedented

Bette's Certificate of Service is now in the collection of the USS Arizona Memorial Museum.

numbers of tourists to Hawaii in the post-war boom, and the greatly expanded visitor industry on Oahu pushed the sugar cane and pineapple industries into the background. Military personnel who had grown attached to Hawaii stayed upon leaving the service, and new neighborhoods sprouted to accommodate a growing population. The quiet, sleepy, somewhat isolated days of Hawaii would never return.

Dorothy Dutton Beach, originally from California but living in Hawaii at the time of the attack, writes, "I remember that as a young girl, living on a ranch in Northern California, I had my own horse. I used to ride down to the beach, taking the German Shepherd with me, look out over the ocean and say, 'Someday I'm going to the Hawaiian Islands!' I loved horses and also wanted to see Texas with its big ranches. I wanted to fly an airplane. Eventually I wanted to get married and have several children, a daughter named Jane with long hair and brown eyes. All my dreams have come true. I feel if you wish for something and work toward that goal, you can achieve it. Sometimes, though, it does take a little extra doing. I had three sons before my daughter, Jane, finally came along! Because I'm an adventurous person, if it hadn't been the WARD for me, it probably would have been something else. I don't think the WARD experience shaped my life any differently."

But for most, the WARD experience had a dramatic effect. "I remember my WARD

Top: *Aloha! Joan Erickson (left front), Monnie Eastwood (right front) and other mainland recruits depart for the west coast.*

Bottom: *Lei-bedecked WARDs smile from the boat deck of the* Monterey.

experience. "I have many, many happy memories of the WARDs. A great group of girls came from the mainland. After the war when Paul was getting out of the Navy and we went back on the old *Permanente,* some of those girls were on the boat with us. I broke down every few hours; it was just like a chapter was closing in our lives and now we were going to face reality and, by God, we did. There was so much intrigue, so much romance, so many marriages that were broken for one reason or another—mostly because you simply didn't know what was going to happen tomorrow, so why not?"

Some of the local WARDs left Hawaii after the end of the War. Suzanne Gould, a "lefty" who had to promise not to poke anyone at the crowded plotting board when she joined the WARDs in 1943, had just completed her training as the first group of mainland recruits arrived. She stayed in her quarters at Ft. Shafter until the end, leaving with the other WARDs on the *Permanente* in August 1945. She comments modestly, "My life really hasn't been outstanding. After leaving Hawaii I worked in Seattle, New York, San Francisco and Ontario, California. Being a member of the WARD was a very enjoyable experience. It did shape the outcome of my life in that it gave me the confidence to be on my own and travel alone."

For the military wives, the end of the war often brought a transfer with their husbands to some new duty station, or a return to the mainland if he elected to leave the service. Kathy Cooper addresses this perspective: "As military wives look back on the years of duty with the WARD, we express a great sense of satisfaction that we were able to do such important war work. We learned from the strength and courage of the women whose husbands or fiances were killed or became missing in action and from the care and support that the staff as well as fellow WARDs showed each woman in all kinds of predicaments. The laughter that we shared brightened and strengthened us then, as well as now."

Of her own departure from Hawaii, Kathy recalls, "In June of 1943, Bud was ordered back to a submarine under construction at New London, Connecticut. I was able to get a release from the WARD, and we left the Islands on a slow transport travelling alone that

experience as a time of great development and exposure," writes *kamaaina* (lifetime Hawaii resident) Lornahope Kuhlman De Clue. "The WARD shaped my life by providing me with the incentive to complete my education. It also impressed upon me the fact that an education without the development of other skills is inadequate preparation for success." Lornahope also notes how close were the bonds that formed. "Although members of the WARD came from different backgrounds, we quickly united and bolstered each other's morale. That way, no matter what our fear, apprehension, heartbreak, or loneliness, we felt we could cope."

Maili Frost Yardley, another *kamaaina,* remembers the emotional impact of the zigged and zagged the whole way across the grey and gloomy Pacific.

"Being a WARD was very important to me. We did vital work, but we could see the funny side of almost any situation and laughed a lot. We knew we were respected and we respected ourselves. We made lasting friendships. Would I become a WARD again, given the same time and place? Most definitely, as fast as possible!"

Military wife Claire Atkins Becker holds a similar opinion. "My WARD experience is unforgettable. I feel closer to my husband, to the Marine Corps, the Army Air Corps and Signal Corps, and to the war in the Pacific. I would not have had it otherwise. I formed a never-dissolved bond with other WARDs and the Army that I never would have had. I still read avidly about the Pacific War in non-fiction and historical novels and relive a good many of those days. As long as we had to have that war, I'm glad I could participate and contribute in some way."

Nell White Larson, who left in January 1943 due to pregnancy, recalls, "My WARD time was the happiest time of the war for me. We shared a sense that we were all in the war together and each one was doing all he could, not only for the war effort, but for those around him. I missed that support and understanding when I waited over three years for my husband after returning to my family."

Happily, WARD Kak Hamlin was eventually reunited with her husband, Hal, following the war's end. Hal had been held as a POW by the Japanese for over three and a half years.

For the mainland recruits, the disbanding of the Women's Air Raid Defense meant the end of their obligation to the Army. To many of them, General Weikert's disbanding of the unit seemed somewhat premature as their contracted travel back to the mainland had not been arranged. Eventually this was worked out and on October 15, 1945 the *Monterey* sailed with a large contingent of lei-bedecked WARDs.

"Until transportation was available to get stateside, some of us worked in a medical clinic as volunteers," Sherry Gerrels Cole remembers. "I worked for a short while in a military finance office, typing, and getting some pay. Our passage home was arranged on the *Mariposa*, a much more elegant ship than the one

on which I went to Hawaii. Since I was planning to get married in San Francisco as soon as Larry got back from Iwo Jima, I was eager to get stateside and get settled. Meanwhile we were allowed to stay in our quarters at Ft. Shafter.

"Horror was the first news we got—in a magazine clipping, I believe—about the concentration camps discovered by our troops in Europe. 'Appalled' was the only description of our feelings about the atomic bombs our country dropped on two Japanese cities, although we couldn't realize the full horror until later— we were jubilant about winning the war.

"My WARD experience certainly did shape my life, and not just by giving me a nickname

Top: Going home are, from left, Beth Lennon, Nancy Haven, Anne Sweet (sitting), Peggy Page and Jackie Sibbald and an identified WARD.

Bottom: Monnie Eastwood (left) and two other "Pasadena Girls" walk up the gang plank to board for their return to California.

that stuck. I met Larry Cole there. In fact, you could say that we were prescribed for each other by my physician, Dr. Kleinfeld, who took care of me during my initial flu. He happened to be Larry's roommate. Once Larry was a bit run down after a mission on some hot, sticky Pacific Island, and the doc invited us both to a small party. Larry, of course, was gone on various military missions most of the time I was on Ft. Shafter, but we stayed in touch and got married after the war. He died in 1971 of a heart attack, just twenty days before our silver wedding anniversary. After that I got involved with a neighbor, Barbara Kerr, because I was fascinated by the interesting devices she had in her back yard. We are now a corporation, Kerr-Cole Inc., and we sell solar ovens, plans and kits. Rich we ain't, but it's exciting! We feel it's really something worth doing, and we're having fun."

"My experience in the WARD gave me distinction in my community," relates mainland recruit Barbara Price Waldrup. "Among friends in Salt Lake City, mine was a singular experience. Growing up in a Mormon community and atmosphere, I was a pretty sheltered girl, yet alone in Hawaii I retained my naivete." Ellen Oros Reed records, "I'm grateful I had the opportunity to be a WARD. Perhaps it did influence the outcome of my life—I know I'm proud to be an American!" Sisters Audrey and Autumn Shade worked for the WARD until the end of the War. "It was a sad time to say goodbye," Audrey writes, "but we were glad the war was over and anxious to see our four brothers who all came home."

Ruth Slaughter Donovan continues to cherish WARD friendships. "I've kept in touch with dear friends from the WARD, and they've seen me through some ups and downs with steadfastness. Our common experiences make nothing that I've done, or could do, unacceptable or something I'd have to hide from them. They already know my worst and best so…what the heck?

"I returned to California for six months after the WARD and 'floundered around' S.F. and Berkeley. Then I went to Manila with the War Crimes Trial and met a gorgeous Major, a paratrooper, on the ship going out. The trip took three weeks and what with romance in the gun turret (no more guns, thank God), we

were more or less engaged by the time we reached Manila. After about six months we were each able to get out of our commitments to the Army, return to California and be married. Several years and three children later we divorced, and I finished raising the children here in the remote mountains of Northern California. Although it didn't last, it was all worthwhile. He died, the children left for college and careers, and I'm still here debating what to do with my life now that I must cut down on gardening, carrying firewood and the other back-breaking facts of life in the mountains. In fact, another ex-WARD who's also alone and I have been talking about joining forces somewhere…but where? How about a WARD retreat for others like me—a Lanikai for us?"

The application of radar was implemented and tested thoroughly by the Signal Corps and the WARD during the war. Today, efforts to remember its significance to the American victory continue. Opana, the first place the U.S. used radar in military action in WWII, was registered as a National Historic Site. In addition, the Honolulu section of the Institute of Electrical and Electronics Engineers (IEEE) nominated the Opana site as an IEEE Electrical Engineering Milestone and unveiled a commemorative plaque on December 6, 1991. Another proposal suggests Opana as the site of a National Radar Park.

Civilian and military engineers and scientists who worked together to expand the functions of radar often claim that radar won World War II and that the atomic bomb merely ended it. Without a doubt, the "Long Range Aircraft Detector and Tracker" and its hundreds of applications have made a dramatic impact on our lives. Radar and radar principles make possible automatic door openers, radar guns to catch speeding drivers, a massive air transportation industry, the exploration of space, even, unfortunately, the capability to guide and control a tremendous network of conventional and nuclear weapons systems. WWII let the genie out of the radar bottle, and WARDs share hope that only beneficial applications will prevail.

By the time that the last shift of WARDs served on September 27, 1945, over six hundred and fifty women had served in the WARD and mainland recruits had represented nearly every state in the Union. Through the years WARD reunions have become not only more frequent and nostalgic, but also, as the official records of the Women's Air Raid Defense were destroyed in a fire at the Federal Personnel Records Center in St. Louis, a crucial tool for keeping alive the history of the organization.

The 45th Anniversary of the Pearl Harbor attack brought approximately a hundred former WARDs plus their spouses and friends to Hawaii, and a dinner held at the Ft. Shafter Officers' Club ended in the impromptu singing of old WARD tunes. A visit by the reunion group to Lizard was covered by the 6:00 o'clock news and the *Honolulu Star-Bulletin*. The reunion ended on Saturday, December 13th, with a Hawaiian *luau* at Pat Swenson's ranch on the North Shore.

WARDs Bette Bellentyne, Kathy Cooper, Nancy Hedemann and Pat Swenson produced a short work entitled *The Women's Air Raid Defense, 1942–1945: A Forty-Fifth Anniversary Report and Roster* in time for the reunion. It summarized the WARD experience and contained a partial listing of WARD members. Copies of the work were made available to the Hawaii State Archives and to State and military libraries.

William and Barbara Boga, who met when she was a WARD, have been in active contact with members of the 7th Fighter Command and the WARDs for many years "due in large part to the late Charlie Price who spent a great deal of his time contacting WARDs and service personnel, arranging reunions, dinners, and get togethers." William, who was the Assistant Adjutant, 7th Fighter Wing, and living in officers' quarters adjacent to those of the WARD, recalls, "The most memorable get together was a reunion in San Francisco to which every WARD and all members of the 7th Fighter Wing and Command who had any connection to us were invited. This was thirty years after the war's end, 1975, and as I recall we had upwards of one hundred in attendance at a dinner held at the Presidio, and

a smaller number at a Ft. Mason luncheon. It was a huge success."

The military is as helpful with reunions as possible. The Public Affairs Office at Ft. Shafter arranged for a group of ex-WARDs to return to Lizard in 1984. The tunnel no longer is used as a plotting center, and visiting "Rascals" were astonished to note that without the balcony, the plotting table, the wall maps, the overhead lights and all the people, the central plotting room seemed unbelievably small. The young soldiers on duty were born long after WWII, but they were curious about wartime use of the tunnel and greeted the WARDs with a large, colorful banner that read, "WELCOME LIZARDS!" The old Rascals forgave them the endearing error.

A half-century ago, as war gripped the entire world, women in Hawaii watched as their homes, their husbands and their families came under Japanese attack. Soon some of these women courageously committed themselves to the work of the Women's Air Raid Defense in hopes that the same tragedy would not happen again. As they fulfilled this personal obligation, they were joined by women seeking adventure and the opportunity to be a part of crucial work for America. In so doing, they earned a place in history for themselves and made a forceful statement about the strength and abilities of women.

Mary Jane Brown (left) and Catherine Harrington (right) wait to board the Monterey *to return to California. Jean Hattori of Honolulu keeps them company.*
Signal Corps, October 13, 1945

Women's Air Raid Defense Roster

OAHU UNIT

Abbott, Lousiana "Weegee"
Leaver, Mrs. Thomas

Adler, Jeanne
Morris, Mrs. William

Ahlborn, Loreen
Nelson, Mrs.

Allen, Eleanor

Amery, Julie
Reese, Mrs.

Anderson, Lucy

Anderson, Palm M.
Outland, Mrs. Gil

Armstrong, June

Argo, Zella B.

Arnold, Shirley
Johnson, Mrs. R. B.

Artiga, Betty
Snipper, Mrs.

Atherton, Burta
Mrs. Frank

Ayer, Jean
Mrs. Frank

Azevedo, Eleanor

Bailey, Margery
Mulkern, Mrs. J. A.

Bailiff, Barbara

Ballentyne, Bette

Baptiste, Lillian
Adams, Mrs.

Barker, Marjorie

Barlow, Barbara
Hanson, Mrs.

Bartlett, Geneva
Zutler, Mrs. Sam

Becker, Claire Atkins
Mrs. Paul E.

Bedford, Janet
Grady, Mrs.

Beier, Dorothea M.
Setliffe, Mrs.

Bell, Elaine Post

Bell, Patricia

Headley, Mrs. Robert

Bellows, Eunice
Mrs. Charles
Nurse

Benson, Lois W.

Bentley, Patricia "Patsu"
Hooper, Mrs. Roger

Berg, Barbara
Boga, Mrs. William J.

Berry, Jane

Berthold, Irene

Bird, Wilma

Biron, Kathleen Shannon

Bischoff, Marjorie
Hass, Mrs.

Black, Dorothy S.

Blaisdell, Marion
Knowles, Mrs. William

Bloomfield, Mildred

Bloomfield-Brown, Bertha
Administration

Bohl, Irene

Bonar, Audrey

Booth, Betty J.

Brenham, Patricia L.

Brennan, Mary B.

Brooks, Iris
Mrs. B. A.

Brown, Mary Jane

Bullard, Mary
Mrs. George

Burke, Darcy
Sutton, Mrs.

Burnette, Dorothy

Burnside, Betty

Calvin, Lillian

Cameron, Barbara

Campbell, Jean

Carlson, Elaine
Esser, Mrs. Nick

Carmalt, Lucy

Carnahan, Helene M.

Carpenter, Juliet Lee "Julie"

Carpenter, Louise L. "Carpy"
Russell, Mrs. Ed

Carter, Eleanor "Flame"
White, Mrs. Larry

Cascioni, Dorothy

Cathcart, Charlotte

Cavanaugh, Anita B.

Champion, Barbara
Veirs, Mrs. Evan I.

Chang, Lorraine

Chapin, Suzette
Tarvornetti, Mrs.

Chesko, Peg

Chilson, Barbara

Chung, Violet

Clark, Vanessie

Clifton, Bessie M.
Mrs. Harvey

Cole, Helen H.
Mrs. Allyn

Coleman, Beth

Coleman, Julia H.

Conklin, Daisy W.
Dunbar, Mrs.

Cooke, Eleanor

Cooke, Elise "Babby"
MacNaughton, Mrs.

Cooke, Nancy Veach
Herrera, Mrs.

Coon, Valeria "Val"
Dotterer, Mrs.

Coonley, Catherine "Kitty"
Supervisor, Oahu Unit

Cooper, Henrietta
Fitzgerald, Mrs.

Cooper, Kathleen Bruns
Mrs. Francis T.

Cope, Ruth
Mrs. W.

Copeland, Barbara

Corbaley, Barbara

Cornwell, Betty J.
Hogoboom, Mrs. William

Cowling, Louise
Nedhoff, Mrs.

Craig, Bernice

Cramer, Barbara
Jackson, Mrs. M.

Crawford, Winona

Cumming, Rita
Knox, Mrs. J. E.

Cummings, Kathryn F.

Curtiss, Mary Salisbury

da Rosa, Vierra
Goldman, Mrs.

Daly, Florence B.

Daniels, Mrs. Betty Isenberg

Davis, Ruth

Delano, Ellen C.

Derx, Charlotte

Deutsch, Leona "Lee"
Kalbacher, Mrs. Frank

Dieter, Maxine

Dillingham, Mrs. Constance S.
Mrs. Gaylord

Dillingham, Mrs. Harriet B.
Mrs. Lowell

Dinker, Marcia Wilson

Downie, Mildred
Freeman, Mrs. Philip

Duborg, Jean H.

Dudley, Maryelise M.

Dulin, Ethylin
Ware, Mrs. Gordon

Dutton, Dorothy "Dottie"
Beach, Mrs. Roy

Eakin, Eleanor H.

Eakin, Margaret

Eastwood, Marian "Monnie"
Lockart, Mrs. Harry

Eddleman, Katheryn

Erdman, Marjorie "Bargie"
Fairbanks, Mrs. Tad N.

Erdman, Mary
Mrs. Harold
Supervisor

Erickson, Joan

Erly, Eleanor

Evans, Dorothy "Presh"
Pattee, Mrs. Burleigh

Finlayson, Mary
Bell, Mrs.

Finley, Arlis

Fisher, Doris

Fiske, Helen
Smith, Mrs.

Flint, Miriam

Foley, Margaret "Maggie"
Jagels, Mrs. George D.

Ford, "Fluff"
White, Mrs. Jack

Forsberg, Karen F.

Fortune, Margaret G.

Fraser, Jean M.
Mrs. Harvey R.

Fraser, Natalie

Fraser, Stella E.
Mrs. Loren

Freed, Annette
Bayless, Mrs.

Frizell, Jane R.

Frost, Maili
Yardley, Mrs. Paul

Frye, Dorothy

Gantt, Virginia
Hunter, Mrs. E. V.

Gaylord, Mary G.

Germain, Barbara
Vredenburgh, Mrs. Jack

Gerrells, Elsa "Sherry"
Cole, Mrs. L. E.

Gilham, Alberta

Gilman, Patricia
Greenwell, Mrs. Raleigh

Gillett, Mrs. Frank G.

Gohl, Betty
Naylor, Mrs. Jack

Gohl, Eleanor
Gilbert, Mrs. Charles

Gordon, Ann
Ward, Mrs. Richard

Gould, Suzanne

Graham, Ruth
Plonski, Mrs. Walter

Greco, Geraldine
Mrs. Joseph

Green, Emmajean O.

Green, Mary M.

Greenwell, Amy

Greenwell, Martha L. "Tommy"
Mrs. James

Gregory, Kathie

Gregory, Martha

Greig, Sioux Hansen
Mrs. Dean

Grismore, Val G.

Gruen, Dolly Jane
Carroll, Mrs. Elliott

Guard, Mildred

Hamilton, Beth

Hamilton, Charlotte B.
Mrs. J. S.

Hamlin, Kathleen L. "Kak"
Mrs. Hal

Hammond, Nancy S.

Hancock, June
Catron, Mrs. Courtney

Handley, Helen D.

Hanes, Margaret J.

Hardaway, Lee H.
Mrs. Robert H.

Harer, Ruth

Harrington, Catherine

Harrington, Ivalee

Harris, Beatrice J.

Harrison, Dorothy

Harrison, Ellebelle L.

Harrison, Janet T.

Hastings, Marjorie
Gray, Mrs.

Haven, Nancy

Hawgood, Virginia "Ginny"
Hartley, Mrs.

Healey, Betty J.

Healy, Marie

Heberling, Tish

Heck, Mildred
Leaman, Mrs. Don

Hedemann, Nancy O.

Hee, Betty

Heffner, Marion K.

Hewett, Joan

Hines, Eleanor

Hitchcock, Barbara
Harris, Mrs. Paul J.

Ho, Betty
Hooper, Mrs. Halden

Hoag, Gloria Z.

Holland, Mary Beth
Hinck, Mrs. Udo

Holmes, Lorraine
Weese, Mrs.

Holt, Patricia J.

Holt, Yvonne A.

Hommell, Eugenia
Hannigan, Mrs. William

Houle, Alice

Howett, Hortensia L.

Hudlow, Grace
Odell, Mrs. Garland

Hyland, Melva M.

In, Bettie O. Y.
Jayne, Mrs. Allen W.

In, Stella Lau

Jennings, Monica
Driscoll, Mrs. Jack

Jennings, Ruth M.

Jensen, Barbara
Marchal, Mrs. G. L.

Jensen, Vernice
Kinney, Mrs.

Johsch, Juanita H.

Jones, Blanche C.

Jones, Elizabeth

Jones, Tilo

Jorgenson, Esther Blue
Lynn, Mrs. Michael

Kadick, Betty B.
Mrs. Misha

Kahake, Grace

Kellett, Margot
McCormick, Mrs. Edward

Kenison, Vera K.
Mrs. Allen

Kilgannon, Moyra

King, Pauahi Carter
Ackerman, Mrs.

Kinnard, Eppy Ann C.

Kinney, Eleanor

Kirby, Lucille
Moffa, Mrs.

Klech, Jean
Mrs. William

Knapp, Mary
Durkee, Mrs. Bill

Knight, Jean S.
Mrs. T. E.

Knouse, Bette
Mrs. Lloyd
Administration

Knudsen, Joyce M.

Kontney, Virginia

Kraul, Dorothy

Kuhlman, Lornahope O.
De Clue, Mrs. R.

Lackey, Laura Jane
Mrs. Raleigh

Landstreet, Helen D.

Lane, Virginia
Atherton, Mrs. James

Langstroth, Lili
Van Rensalaer, Mrs. S.

Langstroth, Virginia S. "Ginny"

Lanser, Tina

Larsen, June

Larsen, Nell White
Mrs. Stanley

Leblond, Joan E.

Lee, Betty Ann

Lee, Helen H.

Lee, Lily N. S.

Lennon, Beth

Lester, Thelma P.

Lim, Sylvia T. M.

Line, Carol

Littlewood, Mary E.

Loughran, Doreen

Love, Martha J.
Hanson, Mrs. Harold B.

Lowrey, Virginia
Brown, Mrs. Zadoc

Lowrie, Charlotte
Rieser, Mrs. Robert

Lowson, Marjorie "Marge"
Simpson, Mrs. Richard

Lum, Ruby Q. S.

Lur, Betty E.

Lyman, Jewell

Lyon, Cecile "Cece"

Lyons, Dorothy
Blackstock, Mrs. Carl

MacKellar, Jean S.

Magoon, Adele W.

Magowan, Doreen

Maher, Marie

Mangelsdorf, Linda
Beech, Mrs.

Marchal, Ruita
Churchill, Mrs. Jordan

Maret, Evelyn A.

Marlowe, Mary
Hogan, Mrs.

Marrow, Jan
Mathews, Mrs.

Martenson, Marjorie T.

Martin, Evelyn

Mather, Kathryn

McArthur, Phyllis "Torchy"

McConnell, Evelyn M.
Mrs. A. W.

McCorkle, Frances "Corky"

McGinnis, Marie
Smith, Mrs.

McGirr, Mary J.

McIntyre, Elinor

McIntyre, Hannah
Jeffrey, Mrs. Robert

McKelvie, Lillian H.

McMaster, Charlotte

McNamara, Lois

McNeill, Barbara C.
Mrs. Paul

Medcalf, Charlotte S.

Menczkowski, Myrtle O.

Mendonca, Mary Louise

Metz, Dorothy
Donahue, Mrs.

Meyer, Dottie
Morrison, Mrs. Lester

Miller, Carolyn C.

Miller, Margaret

Miller, Nancy P.

Mitchell, Katherine

Montgomery, Ruth
Livingston, Mrs. Gordon

Moore, Maxine
Mrs. Ernest

Moores, Adele S.

Moorhead, Peggy

Morgan, Gail

Morgan, J. Patricia "Pat"
Swenson, Mrs.

Morrill, Marjorie

Morse, Jane Loomis
Mrs. Whitney

Mosley, Charlotte A.

Mullen, Marge

Mumm, Lucille K.

Mumper, Peggy Ann
Wilson, Mrs. Billie B.

Nelson, Marge

Neufold, Hester L.
Stubbs, Mrs. S. P.

Norkus, Adele H.

Nye, Sarah E.
Harris, Mrs. Sam

Obenshain, Martha

O'Brien, Evelyn C.

O'Donnell, Doris
Warnock, Mrs. John

Olson, Caroline

Oros, Ellen Reed

Ostrander, Marcella

Ouerback, Jane
Perry, Mrs.

Owens, Jeanne N.

Pabst, Frances

Page, Peggy

Paiote, Peggy

Parker, Margaret Ann

Parker, Maria R.
Terry, Mrs.

Parker, Ruth W. "Woofy"
Mrs. Henry, Jr.

Parks, Betty
Steele, Mrs. Wendell A.

Patrick, Betty P.
McColley, Mrs.

Peacock, Eleanor S.

Peck, Audrey

Pedersen, Isabel

Peed, Margaret

Pekuri, Sigrid

Peterson, Annabelle

Peterson, D. D.

Peterson, Margaret
Dahl, Mrs. G. D.

Pfisterer, Barbara
de Surmont, Mrs. Alain

Pfleuger, Shada
Bryan, Mrs. Ed

Phillips, Patricia

Pickard, Ann "Pick"
McCarry, Mrs. Thomas

Pickerell, Patsy
Jurgensen, Mrs. Earl

Pietsch, Leslie Long
Mrs. David

Pohlman, Helen
Reeves, Mrs.

Poole, Joan
Foley, Mrs. Edward

Powell, Marilyn L.

Pratt, Audrey
Bliss, Mrs. Walter

Pratt, Weymouth

Prewett, Mabel

Prewitt, Flo

Pribnow, Gayle

Price, Barbara
Waldrup, Mrs.

Pritckett, Joyce

Pruett, Jessie

Pulleine, Marjorie

Ramage, Emeleen T.

Ramey, Edna Z.

Redlin, Gerry
Olsen, Mrs.

Reed, Kathleen C.

Reilly, Louise E. "Ouida"
Dunham, Mrs.

Rice, Kathryn M.

Richard, Anabel

Ridings, Dolores

Riebeth, Jane

Ripperton, Margaret
Young, Mrs.

Robbins, Cecile F.

Robinson, Cynthia
Woody, Mrs.

Robinson, Eloise

Robinson, Mary

Roby, Marion K.

Roehm, Rachel M. "Rae"
McDonald, Mrs. Gordon

Roman, Helen Lindsey

Rooke, Virginia

Rose, Ruth Clark

Ross, Leona B.

Rutland, June E.
Mrs. Dale

Salisbury, Jan
McGee, Mrs. Milton

Sawyer, Martha

Scally, Barbara
Armbruster, Mrs. Robert

Scharbach, Eleanor "Blackie"
Hedemann, Mrs. Erling

Schiering, Mary

Schmidt, Jane

Schmitz, Martha

Schwartz, Elaine

Scott, Marie
Howes, Mrs.

Scribner, Sybil
Upton, Mrs. George

Seeband, Mary Myrtle

Shade, Audrey
Cage, Mrs. J. B.

Shade, Autumn
Freeman, Mrs. John

Shaner, Marjorie G.
Gehrig, Mrs.

Sharp, Mary "Bunny"
McKeever, Mrs. Hal

Shaw, Joy B.
Mrs. Sam

Shea, Dorothy Elaine
Mrs. Jack

Shields, Barbara
Washburn, Mrs. W. W.

Shimm, Dora O. Y.

Sibbald, Jackie

Sicher, Dorothy E. "Dottie"
Roberts, Mrs. Thomas E.

Simpson, Dorothy J.
DeBatty, Mrs.

Sims, Ann
Stubenberg, Mrs. Arthur

Sinclair, Patricia

Slaughter, Ruth
Donovan, Mrs.

Slauson, Frances "Fan"
Miller, Mrs.

Slauson, Janet "Bunt"
Rodier, Mrs.

Slye, Ferne
Parish, Mrs. Lucien

Smith, Bettie L.
Mrs. Charles B.

Smith, Donna

Smith, Edythe P.

Smith, Ella Belle
Mrs. Sam

Smith, Gertrude

Smith, Katie
Huber, Mrs. William

Smith, Mabel O.
Christy, Mrs. T. C.

Smith, Marilyn

Smith, Margaret

Smith, Mary Lou

Smythe, Helen
Swanson, Mrs.

Soost, Patsy
Ritter, Mrs.

Spalding, Joan T.

Sperry, Winifred "Bam"
McNaughton, Mrs. M.

Stadtfeld, Audrey P.

Stahl, Grace K.

Stalcup, Lillian
Chambers, Mrs.

Stanley, Fay C.
Shulman, Mrs.

Stevens, Bernice B.

Stevenson, Betty J.

Stewart, Mary
Lowe, Mrs.

Stocker, Wanda J.

Stoker, La Vaughn
Meier, Mrs.

Sumner, Evanita
Midkiff, Mrs. Robert R.

Sweet, Anne

Sykes, Ruth
Mrs. C. S.

Szybolski, Antoinette

Taylor, Ellen
Veach, Mrs. Marshall

Taylor, Flora L.

Taylor, Peggy

Terrelle, Elyse
Lawson, Mrs.

Terry, Muriel

Thies, Caroline

Thompson, Barbara

Thompson, Mary

Thorpe, Lucille

Thrall, Barbara
Mrs. Chester

Thummler, Winifred

Todd, Sandra
Holmyard, Mrs. H. R.

Tom, Geraldine Y. F.

Tower, Louise
Lee, Mrs. Richard

Townsend, Antoinette "Toni"
Hindman, Mrs. Ben

Turk, Leona

Turner, Barbara
Shuttleworth, Mrs.

Tuttle, Mary Jane
McBarnet, Mrs. Alexander

Tuzo, Kathryn E.

Twedt, Mildred
Grimsrud, Mrs. Melvin

Umstead, Thelma Z.
Douglas, Mrs. Robert

Vail, Anne "Betsy"
Mrs. William H.

Van Gieson, Genie
Klein, Mrs. C. E.

Van Gieson, Tina
Sitton, Mrs.

Van Note, Irene

Vanderkloot, Isabel

Vaughn, Gertrude

Wachtel, Ellen

Wagner, Madeline M.

Wainwright, Helen R.

Waldridge, Helen V.

Wallmark, Charlotte

Walthen, M. Eileen

Waltz, Verdelli

Warner, Dee Dee

Warren, Patricia F.

Watts, Virginia "Ginny"
Kjorlien, Mrs. Clarence J.

Waymire, Zelma

Webster, Vera
Biggs, Mrs. Marshall

Weich, Heloise

Weller, Mary Louise "Squeeze"
Case, Mrs. John

West, Janet
Watson, Mrs. Wade A.

West, Katherine

West, Marjorie Mark

Wild, Nancy West

White, Ellin
Burkland, Mrs. Reynolds

Widrin, Tatiana "Tanya"
Brooks, Mrs.

Willett, Marguerita E.

Williams, Daisy
Dunbar, Mrs.

Williams, Gwendolyn
Mrs. Roger
Supervisor, Oahu Unit

Willson, Genevieve
Spiegle, Mrs.

Wilson, Jean E.

Wilson, Louise

Wilson, Marge

Wilson, Marsha

Wilson, Patricia

Wist, Lois
Wright, Mrs.

Witter, Bobbie

Wogen, Corinne
Kahler, Mrs. William

Wolfe, Elsie
Conrad, Mrs. Carroll

Wong, Caroline
Wedemeyer, Mrs. Herman

Wood, Eileen, L.

Woodruff, Marilyn

Wooley, Mary Alice "M.A."
Richards, Mrs.

Worrall, Nancy
Bingham, Mrs. R.

Wuydts, Mary

Yealland, Margaret
Ullstrom, Mrs. William

Young, Audrey
Mrs. G. H.

Zehnder, Edna

HAWAII UNIT

Ah Mai, Ah Ngun
Secretary

Ahuna, Martha
Fisher, Mrs.

Borden, Katherine

Bothelho, Ernestine

Bothelo, Louise

Bush, Hazel
Mrs. Gavin
Supervisor

Cambra, Vivian

Chalmers, Miss

Chan, Betty
Nelson, Mrs.

Chan, Me-Lim

Chee, Mary

Chow, Esther

Choy, Dorothy

Cran, Helen Ann

Decker, Elizabeth

Dosall, Marcella

Edmunds, Elizabeth

Estes, Henrietta

Fergerstrom, Thelma
Teves, Mrs.

Fonner, Marilyn

Freitas, Louise

Gardner, Margaret

Gibson, Betty

Haaunio, Virginia

Hamaku, Winnie

Hohu, Margaret

Hook, Patricia

Kama, Harriette

Kualii, Elizabeth
Afook, Mrs.

Kualii, Sarah
Chun, Mrs.

Lai, Chun Yen

Lee, Florence Chong

Lee, Lois

McSwanson, Mary

Moku, Gladys
Spencer, Mrs.

Moku, Mabel
Obina, Mrs.

Naipo, Helani

Nathaniel, Violet

Notley, Harriette

Palacio, Chris

Palacio, Nellie

Paris, Bertha Herrman

Perez, E.

Perez, I.

Racelis, Aloha
Carvalho, Mrs.

Racelis, Leilehua

Rocha, Velma

Rosehill, Kahiwa

Serrao, Matilda

Simmons, Emmaline

Swain, Ellen

Torrijos, Connie

Victor, Miss

Williams, Mildred Fontes

Wong, Dorothy
Branco, Mrs.

Yap, Amy Aki

Young, Helen Kim
Mrs. Lee

Yuen, Mary Kim

Yuen, Oi Guan

KAUAI UNIT

Ahuna, Mabel

Akana, Kuulei
Akina, Mrs.

Akana, Loretta
Lowrey, Mrs.

Arzador, Pacita

Blacksted, Mabel Kaua

Boiset, Isabel

Bonn, Elizabeth

Castillo, Marie

Ching, Florence
Richardson, Mrs.

Chun, Chin Soon "Chinny"
Mrs. Miles

Costa, Adeline

Costa, Virginia

Crawford, Mrs. Mary
Supervisor

Dang, Beatrice
Wing, Mrs.

Dang, Phyllis
Ching, Mrs.

Dillingham, Alyce

Gomes, Marie

Henriques, Dolores

Henriques, Helen

Kim, Annie

Kim, Kee Soon
Wong, Mrs.

Lowell, Katherine
Hoe, Mrs.

Luke, Iwalani

Luke, Muileen

Lum, Annie
Conching, Mrs.

Lum, Harriet
Mead, Mrs.

Maka, Hattie K.
Holderbaum, Mrs.

McCoy, Elizabeth "Liz"

McGuegan, Florence

Miller, Emma

Montgomery, Hannah

Pa, Violet

Pai, Doris

Palama, Anna

Park, Catherine

Peacock, Marjorie
Supervisor

Rapozo, Carolyn

Rapozo, Jennie

Rente, Eleanor

Rente, Lydia
Viveiros, Mrs.

Rice, Mrs. Flora B.
Mrs. Richard
Supervisor

Samson, Mary
Hendrickson, Mrs.

Schimmelfennig, Dorothy
McKnight, Mrs. William

Smith, Emily

Smith, Lydia

Song, Tamie

Taylor, Thelma
Mrs. Stanley
Supervisor

Tilton, Vivian

Tom, Keale

Valdez, Andrea

Waiau, Pearl D.

West, Lillian

Whang, Marion

Wong, Frances

MAUI UNIT

Aguierre, Lucille
Vierra, Mrs.

Ah Choy, Agnes
Goo, Mrs.

Ah Pang, Jennie

Ah Sing, Caroline A.
Washko, Mrs. Joseph
Supervisor

Alo, Jeanette
Barrows, Mrs.

Anderson, Mary A.
Andersen, Mrs.
Supervisor

Andrade, Emily

Anton, Alma

Asperra, Modesto

Bak, Nancy

Benevides, Gertrude

Bringuel, Agnes
Costa, Mrs.

Cabral, Dorothy
Frerkson, Mrs.

Caires, Adeline
Gouveia, Mrs.

Carvalho, Beatrice
Sister Beatrice, M.M.

Chan, Fannie

Chan-Wa, Stella

Chang, Laura

Ching, Bertha

Chock, Katherine

Choo, Katherine

Costa, Dorothy
Chambliss, Mrs. Joseph

Dang, Myra

Daniels, Evalyn
Nunes, Mrs.

Daniels, Margaret

Dawson, Ruth Vares

Enos, Emily

Enriques, Gladys
Black, Mrs.

Fong, Sophie

Garcia, Virgie

Goo, Marjorie
Wong, Mrs.

Gray, Martha J.
Supervisor

Guililiermo, Jean

Ing, Susan

Johnson, Irene
Pedra, Mrs.

Kam, Myrtle
Hussey, Mrs. Adrian

Kamaka, Bertha
Simonson, Mrs.

Kanekoa, Catherine

Kealohanui, Apolonia K.
Day, Mrs.

Keao, Olga
Han, Mrs. Herbert

Kiakona, Janet
Akau, Mrs.

Kong, Christine
Teruya, Mrs.

Lee, Muriel

Lightner, Amelia
Principal Supervisor

Long, Sophie

Longstaff, Minnie
Mrs. Robert W.

Loo, Marjorie

Marciel, Charlotte
Kuni, Mrs.

Marciel, Pauline
Gregoire, Mrs.

McCaustland, Henrietta
Principal Supervisor

Meyers, Agnes

Milne, Maude

Moniz, Mary

Mookini, Pauline

Mounts, Patricia

Mueller, Eva
Supervisor

Mulligan, Mary

Nobriga, Margaret
Hart, Mrs.

Nobriga, Sylvia

Pali, Myra
Kelupio, Mrs.

Parras, Florence
Kay, Mrs.

Parras, Rachel
Crowell, Mrs.

Robello, Irene
Malson, Mrs.

Rocha, Clytie
Hewlett, Mrs.

Rocha, Eleanor
Watanabe, Mrs.

Roffey, Virginia

Rose, Imogene

Smith, Mrs. Louise
Supervisor

Soffrey, Thelma

Souki, Matilda

Tam Ho, Edith

Tam Wong, Lillian

Tavares, Florence
Teixeira, Mrs.

Tomaso, Helen
Unabia, Mrs.

Tomaso, Sophia
Akina, Mrs.

Vierra, Bernadette
Rodrigues, Mrs.

Vierra, Elizabeth
McCorkle, Mrs.

Waiwaiole, Irmgard

Wong, Katherine